1989

G. K.
CHESTERTON

G. K. CHESTERTON

PHILOSOPHER WITHOUT PORTFOLIO

QUENTIN LAUER, S.J.

FORDHAM UNIVERSITY PRESS
New York
1988

Printed in the United States of America

CONTENTS

Introduction   1

1   Chesterton as Philosopher   5
    PROBLEMS   8
    A PHILOSOPHY OF LIFE   15

2   The Appeal to Reason   25
    RESPECT FOR REASON   26
    REASON AND PARADOX   30
    THE REAL AND THE IDEAL   36
    REASON AND ENTHUSIASM   43
    THE MEANING OF BELIEF   48

3   In Quest of Value   52
    PHILOSOPHY AND TRUTH   55
    CHESTERTONIAN LOVE   60
    MORAL EDUCATION   64
    SUBJECTIVITY AND MORALITY   68
    STABILITY AND CHANGE   75
    THE REFUSAL OF NEGATION   79

4   The Superstitions of Science   84
    SCIENCE AND IDEOLOGY   89
    HUMAN CREATIVITY—FREEDOM   99

5   Social Thought   111
    LOVE OF THE POOR   118
    THE FAMILY   125
    DISTRIBUTISM   131
    CHESTERTON'S "MEDIEVALISM"   139

6   Chesterton's Christian Humanism   147
    THEOLOGY OF THE HUMAN   151
    THE HUMAN NEED OF RELIGION   158

Notes   167
Bibliography   177
Indices   *131,990*   181
    INDEX NOMINUM   181
    INDEX RERUM   183

G. K.
CHESTERTON

INTRODUCTION

IT MIGHT VERY WELL be questioned—by more than one reader
—whether it is still worthwhile to write a book about an
author who, it is true, profoundly influenced Anglo-American
thought in the first four decades of this century, but whose
productivity was so copious that it is difficult to think of it
as of truly lasting value. There is a certain sense in which
such a questioning is justified. As I see it, there is no reason
to write another biography of G. K. Chesterton: that has been
admirably taken care of already. By the same token, so much
has been quite competently written about his literary output
in general—be it his poetry, his novels, his literary criticism,
his biographies, or his contribution to all forms of controversy—that I should consider it rash to try to say something
that has not already been said. Underneath all this, however,
there is a profundity of what I shall dare to call philosophical
thought which can still speak to us—if we are willing to
listen—50 years after Chesterton's death, with a vigor that
has not lost its freshness.

Before I do this, however, it may be necessary to introduce
Chesterton to a readership many of whom have never heard
of him and most of whom have never read him. Let me begin
with an anecdote. Forty-four years ago I taught senior English
in a prestigious Jesuit high school. One of the things I was
determined to do, in my youthful enthusiasm, was to get the
students to write correct—even if not necessarily elegant—
English. With a view to this, one of the things I did was to
have them take ten minutes to write a paragraph every morning of the week. Believe it or not, I corrected every one of
those paragraphs, all thirty-five of them, every night—once
more, youthful enthusiasm kept me going. Then, each Monday, I went over a selected number of these paragraphs, pointing out errors, even infelicities of style. Incidentally, the end

1

result of all this was predictable—in a double sense. (1) At the end of the year there was a marked improvement in the students' writing—grammatically, stylistically, and even imaginatively. (2) During the following summer a number of the same students wrote me personal letters. The majority were back where they began, at square one; good writing, apparently, was not for personal letters!

One Monday morning during the year I told the students that, before commenting on their writing I would read them an essay written by a 15-year-old boy. As I read the essay I could see their eyes pop and their jaws drop. As I finished reading I said to them, "That essay, gentlemen, was written by a fifteen-year-old boy named Gilbert Keith Chesterton"; to which the unanimous response was, "Oh well, what do you expect? It's not fair." To which my reply was, "Nevertheless, he *was* only a 15-year-old boy, and what a 15-year-old boy—even if a genius—can do, 18-year-old boys could at least aspire to do."

Why am I relating this story? My first point is that their response indicated clearly that these high-school seniors not only knew who G. K. Chesterton was but had also at least sampled some of his writings. I venture to predict that if one were to try the same trick today—even in a prestigious Jesuit high school—very few, if any, of the students would know who G. K. Chesterton was, and none would have read anything he had written—with the possible exception of a few who had read one or the other of the Father Brown mystery stories, which are still relatively popular. Try the same experiment today with college seniors—even seniors in a Jesuit college—and I venture to say the results would be similar, even though they *might* have heard of Chesterton's name.

But the story is not over. I have recently had occasion to speak with college teachers—at Fordham University—who have Ph.D.s in areas other than English, philosophy, or theology, and who have never heard of Chesterton, and, *a fortiori*, have not read him. More than that, it is quite likely that, if you speak with any contemporary teachers between

2

the ages of 35 and 50, no matter what their specialty, you will find *some* who have never heard of Chesterton, and *most* who have never read anything of his—but, I suppose, the same could be said of Robert Browning, Samuel Johnson, or William Makepeace Thackeray!

The answer in all of this could, I suppose, be that I am the one who has wasted time devoting many years of my life to research in the thought and writing of a has-been, whose writing is so dated, that it is of only antiquarian interest. (That, by the way, is what David Hume said about Aristotle, who is read today far more widely than is Hume!) My contention, however, will be that, although G. K. Chesterton wrote much that today is dated and need not be read, some of it even trivial, nevertheless, the continued profundity of his thought and the aptness of the manner in which he expresses it eminently repay reading him in large doses. I should perhaps mention that my own acquaintaince with Chesterton goes back a very long way—I hesitate to say how long—to when my maiden aunt, an ardent devotee of G. K. Chesterton, had me reading Chesterton's *Heretics* in the seventh grade (I have since had to read the same book four times and have not plumbed *all* its depths yet). There might, nevertheless, be doubts in more than one mind about the justification for calling G. K. Chesterton a "philosopher." To such minds, I am sure, the fact that Chesterton never earned a doctorate—that he never even attended a university—precludes the possibility of his being called a philosopher in any but a metaphorical sense. Philosophically speaking how could such a relatively uneducated—or self-educated—man have anything worthwhile to say? What philosophical audience could he have? Many of his friends and commentators, chief among them Maisie Ward, regret that he chose to remain all his life a "journalist," when he could have become an outstanding literary figure; the implication in this being that the options were journalist *or* "literary figure," not "philosopher." To all of which the only answer is that genius cannot be tied down to the rules of the academy, nor need we be subservient to the prejudices of the academy in evaluating genius. Chesterton, in fact, chose to be a journalist, because in that role he could think most profoundly, powerfully, cogently, and effectively. Most of us, I am sure, are aware that the chief advantage of having a doctorate is that we do not have to be impressed by anyone else who has a doctorate.

Nothing of what I have said up to this point, obviously, proves anything. It may very well be true that, in 1944, especially in a Catholic and Jesuit school, there was every reason why students should not only know *about* G. K. Chesterton but also have read enough of his incredibly voluminous writings to be genuinely *familiar* with him not only as a writer but also as a profound thinker whose influence during the first three decades of the twentieth century was colossal. That by itself does not say that I should today be recommending a familiarity with the thought of G. K. Chesterton, not only to students, whose minds are in the process of being formed, but also to mature scholars who are interested in being as human as possible—but that is precisely what I intend to do.

1

Chesterton as Philosopher

NOT INFREQUENTLY, when I speak to people, including my own colleagues, about my interest in making Chesterton's thought better known, I am met with what seems to be becoming a stock remark, "But you are a philosopher; why are you interested in Chesterton?" The implication, it would seem, is that G. K. Chesterton was primarily a "journalist"—which, by his own admission and even preference, he was—and that that precluded the possibility that he could make philosophers sit up and take notice. I might add here, by way of a sort of parenthesis, that there are any number of outstanding—even great—philosophers who today will not make certain contemporaries who call themselves philosophers sit up and take notice. I do not expect to be speaking to them at all. I once actually heard a young graduate student in philosophy *boast* that he had never read a word of A. N. Whitehead! That, however, is not exactly to the point. The real question is whether there is anything about the thought of Chesterton which should recommend it precisely to philosophers. Many of my friends concur in telling me that this is a giant step down from Hegel! There are few who would deny, even today, that Chesterton was a brilliant essayist who confronted with consummate skill the issues—particularly the moral issues—of his day. This very fact, however, we will be told, stamps a date on his essays, making it a waste of time to read them today, as though one could stamp a date on moral issues—or on moral reasoning—which, by the way, Chesterton considered the very heart of philosophical thinking. How many are there today who read Chesterton's contemporaries, e.g., Hilaire Belloc, Christopher Dawson, Maurice Baring, George Bernard Shaw, H. G. Wells—except perhaps as English literature: for example, the still popular plays of Shaw? G. K. Chesterton is alive and kicking today—in a way that most of his contemporaries are not—precisely because he enunciated clearly and forcefully the fundamental principles in the light of which issues, whether of today or of yesterday, can be confronted intelligently. By the same token there are few, I imagine, who will question the renown of Chesterton as literary critic; his studies of Charles Dickens, Robert Browning, Chaucer, Blake, and Stevenson are scarcely to be surpassed. His biographies, particularly of Francis of Assisi and Thomas Aquinas, must still be called masterful; his novels, despite the fact that he himself was not quite content with them, are still worth reading. His verse, some of which can be dignified with the august name of poetry, still has a strong drawing power. There is a very real sense in which he is a master of Christian apologetics—even though one might wish to bring him up to date on some of that—and no one, I trust, disputes that his three specifically philosophical works, *Heretics*, *Orthodoxy*, and *The Everlasting Man*, have a power which does not wane with time. Whether these books are works of philosophy, making Chesterton a philosopher, is, of course, another question, which demands that we be very cautious in our approach to the thought of Chesterton. To write or speak *about* anyone's thought is to run the risk of systematizing it, and, in the case of Chesterton, this would be to falsify it; and this is one of the reasons why it is so difficult to write about Chesterton's thought, which resists systematization. There is, however, a sense in which Chesterton's thinking *is* systematic; not in the sense that one can logically derive all his ideas by systematically working out the principles from which he begins—he is no Aristotle or Aquinas or Spinoza or Hegel—but in the sense that his view of reality is consistently holistic, literally *seeing* the interrelatedness of all reality in such a way as to see the unreality of the partial if it ceases to be organically connected to the whole. His prodigious memory, which he saw as a gift from God, and for which he was grateful, contributed greatly to his ability to see in this way. He never forgot anything he experienced—although he could readily forget where he was supposed to be at a given time. He read voraciously in his youth and never forgot what he read—although he drove punctilious scholars mad by his tendency to forget the exact wording of what he remembered and to refuse to take time out to look it up. His mind was too constantly busy for that. This is one of the reasons why he is not always easy to follow: there is no way of knowing where he is going when he starts out. At the same time there is nothing of a "stream of consciousness" in this; he knows the *reasons* for the connections he *sees*, even though it may be difficult for us to see how he goes from here to there, or to match the rapidity with which he does it. Perhaps what we should say here is that Chesterton was not a philosopher in the sense of one who, like Plato or Aristotle, Aquinas or Bonaventure, Descartes or Kant, Hegel or Kierkegaard, made original contributions to the history of human reflection on the reality of the real. We can, however, say that he made two remarkable contributions which are still immensely worthwhile today: (1) he was unmatched in his ability to satirize the philosophical foibles of his day; and (2) although his philosophy was not unique his manner of expressing it was unique; one cannot read him, even today, without being again and again suddenly pulled up short. In view of his perennial concern with ideas—and with ideas that count, with ultimates—he has to be called a philosopher, not merely, however, as a lover of wisdom, but as one who possessed a certain kind of intuitive wisdom.

PROBLEMS

The time has come, it would seem, to speak of the difficulties involved in attempting to present the thought of Chesterton—difficulties which all who have attempted to do so have experienced. To begin with, his mind is so sharp and his field of vision so vast that the task of capturing his thought is like that of covering an entire age rather than just the thought of one man. He himself, incidentally, was unable to write an autobiography, in the accepted sense of that term, because he could not be tied down to a sequential account of his life. He could only portray the meanderings of a mind which was always moving toward one and the same goal—but not always in a straight line. At the same time he was unable to avoid the autobiographical which crops up in everything he wrote —in a certain sense all the characters he writes about turn out to be himself. His understanding of them is his self-understanding, and as he enables us to understand them we gradually come to understand him.

Then there is the problem of style. How is one to capture the man who was Chesterton without capturing the style in which the man wrote? And how capture the style in which he wrote without having the mind behind that style? Simply to attempt to write the way he does is to court disaster, to run the risk of artificiality—a risk many a Chestertonian has failed to escape. If one were to try to say what Chesterton says in a style less epigrammatic, less paradoxical, less illustrated by brilliant parallels than his is, one would be condemned to seeing the whole thing fall flat. Whereas, on the other hand, to borrow from him these tricks of style, which for him are so natural, is to become inevitably artificial. Most of us simply do not see the way he sees and should not pretend to do so—although he does have a way of enabling us to see, after reading him, better than we did before. Strictly speaking, he does not teach; he simply enables us to see. We inevitably come away from reading him seeing more cogently than we did before—which does not *have* to mean agreeing with him. No one knew better than Chesterton himself that constant agreement and nothing but agreement is stifling.

Even granting all this, it still seems necessary for me to say without, I trust, too much bathos what I mean by calling Chesterton a philosopher—even though it be "without portfolio." The first thing to say, perhaps, is that Chesterton was by no stretch of the imagination a student of philosophy, a professional philosopher—which may well be the reason he is still worth reading. With the exception of St. Thomas Aquinas, whom he read rapidly and digested remarkably well in the process of writing what has to be one of the best books ever written about the great medieval Scholastic, finding in him much of what Chesterton had already thought out for himself, his knowledge of other philosophers was at best very sketchy. He had a nodding acquaintance with Plato and Aristotle, effectively recognizing their timelessness, from time to time borrowing from them, but never plumbing their depths. He remembered what any English schoolboy would have read of Descartes, Spinoza, Bacon, Hobbes, Locke, Berkeley, and Hume, although he speaks of them but sparingly. He was also completely misinformed with regard to Kant, Hegel, Marx, Kierkegaard, and Nietzsche, although he did manage to make pentratingly true remarks about each of them. In short, his acquaintance with philosophy as systematic discipline is at best rudimentary; but the power of his own rational thinking and his capacity to express it is astounding. Here, however, it is necessary to enunciate a number of cautions. (1) Although Chesterton speaks again and again of the need of logical thinking, he does not make the mistake of taking rational thinking and logical thinking, at least in the formal sense, to be either synonymous or co-terminous. (2) If Chesterton's thinking is to be categorized at all, it might aptly be termed "intuitively rational"—*seeing* connections rather than *deducing* them, even though he constantly speaks of "deduction" and "syllogistic reasoning" as characterizing his own thinking. (3) This brings us to the question of whether Chesterton's "rational" arguments can be used against him. If by "rational argument" is meant "proof" in the strict sense of the word, the answer has to be yes, precisely because only the acceptance of his overall world-view makes it imperative to accept any particular argument of his. There is a very important sense in which it is true that Chesterton never "proves" anything (which is not to say that he has no extraordinarily cogent arguments); he makes one *see* what is the rational thing to affirm. "For the very few things that are really worth believing are not worth proving."[1] Frequently enough the best reason he can give for holding a position to be true is the simple fact that "ordinary" human beings consistently consider it to be true. (4) It is very important to make a clear-cut distinction—which is not always done—between the irrational (contra reason) and the non-rational in regard to Chesterton's thinking. It is never irrational, but it is frequently non-rational, at least in the sense of non-rationalistic or not formal-logically compelling. If we want a technical term to characterize Chesterton's thinking, we might call it "speculative" (to borrow a term from Hegel), in the sense of a thinking-into and a thinking-through. Although there is nothing of Romantic intuitionism in Chesterton, there is a strong element of vision, of "seeing" rationally. If we want to speak non-technically, perhaps the term "sane" (or "sound") tells us more about his thinking than does the term "rational."

It would seem that the best way to characterize G. K. Chesterton's thought is to recognize it as pre-eminently "common sense," which he himself calls "that instinct for the probable,"[2] and which Cardinal Newman, perhaps more systematically, recognizes as an ability to be convinced by the "convergence of probabilities." There can be no question that Chesterton was thoroughly convinced that there is something we can designate as "certainty" and that the human mind is capable of attaining to certainty, provided the concept of certainty not be confined to mathematical truth or to that which is apodictically demonstrable. If all we can affirm with certainty are such truths as these, sanity will not be long in passing us by. Chesterton's "certainty," on the other hand, is what no "sane" person will doubt, whether it be the persistent object of sense perception, or the rational truths to which pure thought attests.

What we are being called on to do, then, is perhaps to make the attempt to understand Chesterton by asking ourselves precisely what he was trying to do. If we read as much as we possibly can of what he wrote, we shall, I think, agree with his brother Cecil who said many years ago: "He is primarily a propagandist, the preacher of a definite message to his own time,"[3] even though it might be contended that the primacy of propaganda and the profundity of philosophical thought seem to be in conflict. In the context, it should be quite obvious, "propaganda" need have no pejorative connotations whatever; by dint of constant profound thinking Gilbert had convinced himself of a number of fundamental truths which were of significance for the leading of an authentic human life. He was convinced, too, that the best he could do for his fellow humans, to express his love for them, was to get them to think in such a way that they would see these truths as clearly as he did. In so doing he was seeking to spread, to "propagate" these fundamental truths and thus get people to think clearly about what is important, about the meaning of human life, about the glory and excitement of existing as human. "The deepest of all desires for knowledge," he insisted, "is the desire to know what the world is for and what we are for."[4] Playing on Hamlet's "To be or not to be, that is the question," he assures us that St. Thomas Aquinas replies with a voice of thunder, "To be, that is the answer."[5] To speak this way to a world which had already experienced one world war and which was about to slide into another was to proclaim, frequently to deaf ears but always with a live voice, that there is a purpose to existence, a purpose to life. It was also to relate any truth whatsoever to the meaning of human life, and to do that is to think philosophically, to make sense out of being human. Here, however, we come up with a problem regarding Chesterton, a problem that will not go away. For the most part we assume that when people say something they mean what they say, and, when the speaker in question is a Chesterton, that he knows what he means. The assumption, however, need not always be literally justified—we all know that those who insist, usually vociferously, that one say exactly what one means are, to say the least, annoyingly boring. Often enough, when someone speaks, even if that someone is as profound a thinker as Chesterton, the speaking is as much a seeking after meaning as it is a proclamation of meaning found. It is for this reason that it is frequently most difficult to make unqualified statements as to what Chesterton meant. Sometimes, for example, he could take an expression, which could have any number of meanings, all of them vague, and write a whole brilliant essay attacking one of its possible meanings. How often, for example, we say to someone on a holiday, "Enjoy yourself," meaning by that "have a good time." Chesterton will play upon that expression, giving it a meaning it does not really have, and thus tell us that we can enjoy wine, or sports, or entertainment, but not ourselves, which would be too introverted. In travestying the meaning of the expression he is making a valid and important point. By the same token Chesterton violently attacks an expression such as "That young man believes in himself," by deliberately ignoring the more probable meaning of "believes in himself," and taking it as though it were saying, "I am the one I believe in," which is patent and arrogant nonsense. Not infrequently, in fact, Chesterton attaches any number of possible meanings to very common expressions, simply in order to get a truth across strikingly.

None of what I am saying here, obviously, is to be interpreted to mean that we cannot come to grips with what Chesterton means—even though it might well take more than one reading to fathom all he means, including his double meanings. What one says of Chesterton may very well be true, but only on condition that one be ready to see that the opposite may also be true. Perhaps the best way to characterize Chesterton's writing style is to say that it is torrential; it flows with great force but also with great ease, such that the ease can disguise the force, and the force can disguise the ease (as though the ease were to be seen as mechanical)—and both can disguise the direction of the thought behind the style, which thought is always quite definite. Reading Chesterton is an intellectual experience not unlike the emotional experience of contemplating Niagara Falls—the experience of force, of irresistibility, but not of chaos; we remain in control of our own response. According to Maisie Ward, "Chesterton often said that in unfolding his fundamental philosophy he could begin anywhere, from potatoes or policemen, from an umbrella to a hansom cab."[6] This in itself need not be confusing, but we do have to be on our toes to follow him in making the connections he makes. Any conceivable object, a piece of string, a man running after his hat, a Gothic arch in a cathedral, or a hippopotamus in the zoo, could set Chesterton's mind moving at an incredibly rapid pace, ultimately leading him, and us with him, into the profoundest thoughts about human life, about God, about the Church, about the universe, without our having a feeling of having been tricked. There are those, of course, who find it little short of frivolous to write of weighty philosophical matters in an amusing and entertaining as well as a striking way, although no one has managed to establish, philosophically or otherwise, that profundity and solemnity are inseparable.[7] Christopher Hollis states the case very succinctly when he says, "Chesterton, though deeply rational in his conclusions, was pictorial and romantic in his manner."[8] In this he was almost unique. I say "almost unique," because, strangely enough, he was equalled—if not surpassed—in this by Nietzsche, whom Chesterton consistently failed to appreciate, if ever he even gave himself the chance to appreciate him.

This seems to be the place, by the way, to lay to rest the suspicion entertained by not a few that Chesterton was simply impractical, concerning himself far more with ideas than with action. If by this is meant that Chesterton could scarcely tie his own tie or remember where he was supposed to be at a given time, there may be a trivial sense in which the statement is true. If, on the other hand, it means that he devoted too much of his time to thinking and not enough of it to doing, it is exasperatingly nonsensical. Not only is doing divorced from thinking more than likely to be irresponsible, it is almost bound to be highly impractical, for if action is to be worthwhile we must know both what we are doing and why we are doing it. It can, of course, be said that G. K. Chesterton did contribute more to ideas than to action, but so does any philosopher. Chesterton himself has put it rather neatly: "You cannot turn a thing upside down, if there is no theory about when it is right way up."[9] Theory, after all, is frequently more practical than practice. There was a joke that circulated in France about a half-century ago about a Frenchman, a German, and an American faced with a serious problem. The Frenchman, it was said, would give a brilliant speech on the subject, the German would write a profound book, and the American would *do* something about it—even though he did not quite know what he was doing. Chesterton thought out profoundly what *ought* to be done.

A PHILOSOPHY OF LIFE

There is a danger, we have to admit, that in putting so much emphasis on Chesterton the thinker we may run the risk of distorting the image of G. K. Chesterton as a human being. There is, for example, the almost universal agreement among those who knew him that he was from his earliest years right down to his death a *good* person in the very strongest sense of the term "good." Most of us, I am sure, will be willing to admit that there are very few people we have known of whom it can be said simply and without qualification that they were just plain good, that they were supremely *good-at* being just what a person ought to be. Cyril Clemens, in his *Chesterton as Seen by His Contemporaries*, and Maisie Ward, in her *Return to Chesterton*, quote large numbers of testimonials to the sheer goodness of G. K. Chesterton as a person. It could be summed up in the words of Father O'Connor (Brown): "It was part of his philosophy, that unfailing consideration for others."[10] One could say that at the root of his goodness was his extraordinarily acute awareness of the need to be grateful for the abundant gifts that make up both the mystery and the exhilarating experience of life, of existence. It was precisely this awareness of the miracle which is life that prevented him from ever taking life *for* granted and at the same time made him intensely conscious of life *as* granted, as a gift, for which the only adequate response is gratitude; he called it "the idea of taking things with gratitude and not taking things for granted";[11] I venture to say that what characterized Chesterton more than anything else was his sense of gratitude; it was precisely that which led him inevitably to the affirmation of the reality of one personal Being to whom it made sense to be grateful; it made no sense to be thankful to Nature, a metaphorical anthropomorphic being that could neither give nor not give because not free. One might look upon nature as a mode of the giving that characterizes the personal Being we call God, but nature cannot be a substitute for the giver of gifts, even if one spells the word with a capital N. One might want to call the need to thank a psychological need, but it is sheer arbitrariness to refuse to recognize that the need to thank is also a need imposed by logic itself, provided the logic in question be human and not merely mathematical. Chesterton himself refers to a kind of mystical logic, which can be quite imperious; the excitedness of existence, the appreciation of which is exuberant: "my original and almost mystical conviction of the miracle of existence and the essential excitement of all experiences."[12] Gratitude was not to be reserved for special occasions; it was to be a constant accompaniment of life, particularly of the lives of the highly gifted.

> The universal objection to the people who are proud of genuine calibre is not any mere jealousy of them; it is not a paltry or panic-stricken resentment of their admitted superiority. It is, like a great many other things which ordinary people feel in a flash and could not possibly defend, entirely philosophical. The instinct of the human soul perceives that a fool may be permitted to praise himself, but that a wise man ought to praise God. A man who really has a head with brains in it ought to know that this head has been gratuitously clapped on top of him like a new hat. A man who by genius can make masterpieces ought to know that he cannot make genius. A man whose thoughts are as high as the stars ought to know that they roll almost as regardless of his power [sic]. A man who possesses great powers ought to know that he does not really possess them.[13]

It is precisely because Chesterton contends that to respond in this way to existence is rational, that the gratitude of which he speaks often has to be seen as part and parcel of his philosophy, which was an unceasing inquiry into why things are the way they are and into how they ought to be. As he saw it, virtue and rational self-determination were inseparable. To those who do not share Chesterton's convictions, of course, it could seem quite arbitrary—and, therefore, not rational—that Chesterton's all-pervading sense of the need to be grateful for all the wonders of existence should force him to affirm the reality of an infinite, personal Giver to whom he could be thankful. To this, of course, Chesterton's answer would undoubtedly be that the arbitrariness and irrationality are all on the other side. His sensitivity here, incidentally, may explain why his two most successful biographies were lives of saints, Francis of Assisi and Thomas Aquinas. If there is one quality that characterizes every saint there is, it is the tremendous sense of gratitude which results in living one's life and in giving that life in thankfulness. Chesterton seems to have perceived with a special sort of acuteness the relation of sanctity and thankfulness. Perhaps one has to *be* a saint to experience the joy of *having* to be thankful to another, even if that other be God. *Having* to be thankful, after all, *can* be embarrassing. Without canonizing Chesterton, might we not say that it takes a very special kind of person to recognize as keenly as he did the connection between thankfulness and sanctity, which he portrays so well in these two books? Chesterton himself had no psychological fear—or resentment—of the dependence which gratitude expresses. Perhaps the best we can do is to recognize that there are some who see so clearly that they are capable of being everlastingly thankful for the inestimable gift of existence and, perhaps, the gift of seeing clearly. Thinking and thanking, after all, can scarcely be separated. As Chesterton puts it with his usual succinctness: "It is the root of all religion that a man knows he is nothing in order to thank God that he is something."[14] It is precisely because Chesterton did see this so clearly that he also saw that the real separated from the totality of reality is ultimately not real at all and thus that he could see that philosophy without theology is ultimately meaningless, or perhaps, as Hegel puts it, "philosophy *is* theology," and only as such does it make sense. This, in turn, implies that Chesterton's philosophical reflections are inseparable from his religious convictions—although by a peculiar sort of reversal his philosophical reflections and the conclusions derived therefrom seem to precede his affirmation of many of these conclusions as religious truths, witness *Heretics* and *Orthodoxy*. Theology, in this context then, becomes rational reflection on the truths precisely as religious, without which theological reflection philosophy itself becomes inadequate. His philosophy, after all, need not be any the less philosophical for being religious—even for advocating religious commitment as being indispensable to being authentically human.

Here it is, however, that Chesterton's view of philosophy—even his use of the term—differs considerably from the more technical understanding of the term when it is employed by some professional philosophers, for whom the term "philosophy" is reserved for an inquiry that is restricted to the purely natural function of reason; for Chesterton the merely natural could never be adequately human. In Chesterton's view, because reason functioning purely naturally—assuming as its advocates presumably do that reasoning is a function of nature and not uniquely a function of spirit—cannot come to terms with the totality of reality. A philosophy grounded in purely natural reasoning, therefore, cannot but be inadequate, even as philosophy. None of which prevents him, incidentally, from putting enormous stress on reason and rationality. In so doing, however, he puts far less stress on the mechanics of narrowly logical thinking than he does on the truth of the conclusions arrived at by a thinking, which is adequately rational; we might call this the *objective* rationality of what is thought, as distinct from the *subjective* ratiocination of the thinking process. Here it is that Chesterton's conviction that reasoning can never be simply "doing what comes naturally" is of such extraordinary importance.

It is for this reason, perhaps, that it was inevitable that Chesterton should have become a Christian and, ultimately, not only a Christian but a Roman Catholic. He saw clearly that in the Christian tradition it simply never made sense to speak of a human being as simply a being of nature; a spiritual being *in* nature, yes, but no *more* than a natural being, no. Straight thinking simply cannot think that. Since in this his own thinking fit right into the Christian tradition, it was no giant step to the realization that his own mind and thinking had roots in that tradition which, he was convinced, had formed the English mind. The next step, it would seem, was equally inevitable, even though it took a much longer time to mature. It was the gradual realization that the only way to make sense of the English Christian tradition was to see it as Roman Catholic England's tradition. Ultimately then, for Chesterton, coming to the Catholic Christian faith was a coming home; it was the ultimate reconciliation of the natural and the supernatural, without which he could make sense of neither. The faith of his fathers answered the deepest needs of his being. When asked why he believed, he answered quite simply, "Because I perceive life to be logical and workable with these beliefs, and illogical and unworkable without them."[15] It is definite convictions, strangely enough, which contribute to the agility of the mind and to the movement of thought.

There is a sense, then, in which for Chesterton his "philosophy" consists of the sum-total of his definite convictions, the convictions that make a difference as to how he looks upon life and how he lives it, whether these convictions be religious, social, ethical, metaphysical, or aesthetic, such that no matter where he begins to think the whole of his "philosophy" is involved. It is for this reason that we can assert that in Chesterton's view a philosophy which is not a philosophy of the human is not adequately philosophical and a philosophy which is a philosophy of the human only is not adequately rational. It is for this reason, too, that what he calls his *Autobiography* is not, as such writing ordinarily is, an account of the events of his life, as it is the unfolding of the process of his thinking. This sort of thing will make sense only if the mind that does the thinking is open, but nothing will be accomplished if all it does is stay open. In the *Autobiography* G. K. Chesterton compares himself to H. G. Wells in these words: "I think he [Wells] thought that the object of opening the mind is simply opening the mind. Whereas I am incurably convinced that the object of opening the mind, as of opening the mouth, is to shut it again on something solid."[16] That, of course, has its risks, since it is based on the antecedent conviction that what the mind shuts on will be something solid, which it may well be, but the shutting does not necessarily make solid what the mind shuts on. There is, however, a kind of parallel here with Chesterton's discovery of religious faith as that which gives solid meaning to life. Accompanying it was a realization that reliance on reason is itself an act of faith in reason, precisely because there are no rational grounds for demanding that reality should function as reason dictates, which did not make him popular with "rationalists." If nothing else this precludes the necessity of being unhappy when an appeal to "nature"—or to natural explanation—does not succeed in solving all the mysteries of the cosmos. Like any other Christian, Chesterton had the tremendous advantage over the atheist, the materialist, the naturalist, that he was free to believe or not to believe in, say, a miracle. The others were *obliged* to disbelieve, because their *dogma* will permit nothing else.

Part and parcel of faith in reason, of course, is the realization that reason is trustworthy only if it refuses to lose contact with facts and in its thinking relies on what he calls "strong, undisputed first principles."[17] Neither facts nor principles can be "proved"; they are the preconditions for whatever proof is to be; one either sees them or one does not. One either sees, for example, that human nature is superior to all the rest of nature, or one does not, and one's entire view of reality depends on whether one sees that or not. Among the things that many of Chesterton's admirers prize so much in him is his ability to enliven the most serious argumentation with a manner that is humorous, entertaining, paradoxical, wildly illustrative, and replete with puns. Those who dislike Chesterton do so for approximately the same reasons—in addition to their not liking his opinions. There is no need, of course, to deny that Chesterton sometimes overdoes this sort of thing, that sometimes his pyrotechnics become tedious—perhaps even counter-productive—that he sometimes substitutes a destruction of his opponent's position by ridicule for serious establishment of his own position, but what both his admirers and his detractors sometimes miss is the role these manners play in making us *see* the truth rather than *proving* it logically—especially where logical proof is not where things are at. An argument, after all, is not less solid because it is illustrated amusingly or interestingly, and more often than not the witty paradox or illustration startles us into seeing the truth that logical demonstration would only obscure or render uninteresting. To state that it would never occur to anyone with even half a brain that the reindeer in pre-historic southern France drew pictures of themselves on cave walls gets its point across more effectively—and at the same time more amusingly—than any disquisition on the reasoning powers of the human brain, especially as the human brain has no reasoning powers whatever, no more than the concert master's violin has the power to play itself. The question is not whether one *likes* humor, paradoxes, or puns; rather it is whether they get done what

the author wants them to do and whether Chesterton
would have been who he was and what he was, if he had
tried to get his point across in more long-faced ways.
There is no question that his brilliance is never a cold
brilliance, precisely because he is always so earnest, but
his brilliance is brilliance nevertheless.

When all this has been said, it would be less than
honest not to admit that there is a certain temptation,
which not all Chestertonians have succeeded in overcom-
ing, to translate an appreciation of Chesterton's accom-
plishment into a cult of his person, the sort of cult that
permits no negative criticism of what he has done. It is
the sort of thing that occurs far less now than it did when
he was the knight in shining armor going forth daily to
do battle for an embattled Catholic minority in England,
Canada, and the United States. For this group of "professional Catholics," as Ian Boyd calls them, "Chesterton
is an institution to be defended rather than an author to
be discussed. A characteristic which defines their attitude
is an aggressive defensiveness towards him as a writer who
needs their protection combined with an astonishing ignorance and uncertainty about the writing they are trying to protect."[18] Chesterton's effectiveness as a thinker,
a controversialist, a propagandist, and a philosopher, does
not and will not depend on his being considered a great
literary artist, a great poet, a great novelist—not even a
great philosopher in the most significant sense of that
term, although it might depend on his being what Ernst
Bloch, an outstanding German Marxist philosopher,
hardly prejudiced in favor of Chesterton's views, called
"einer der gescheitesten Männer, die je gelebt haben"[19]
(one of the most intelligent men who have ever lived).
Bloch, it would seem, speaks this way, precisely because
of Chesterton's paradoxical mode of expression (his dia-

lectic) and his consistent opposition to capitalist greed. He had his weaknesses, his blindnesses, his prejudices, and yet he *was* great (perhaps we should say a "great journalist," in the best sense of that term), but he was not perfect: no merely human being is.

2

The Appeal to Reason

IN HIS EULOGY OF CHESTERTON delivered at the funeral
Mass on June 27, 1936, Monsignor Ronald Knox said,
"All our generation has grown up under Chesterton's influence so completely that we do not even know when we
are thinking Chesterton."[1] That generation, of course, is
no longer with us, but there is a generation, my own, upon
whom that influence was almost equally powerful, a generation that can understand what Knox was talking about.
This is not to say that it is easy for us today to put ourselves back in our formative years, when the living Chesterton was on the scene and when it was impossible for
the intellectually curious not to be influenced by him—
one way or another. It is difficult for us who were then
under that influence to say what it was. A good many of
us, of course, tried to imitate him, especially the flow of
ideas, the paradoxical style of writing, the always apt
parallels and illustrations, the ease with which anything
whatever could remind him of whatever he wanted to be
reminded of. High school and college newspapers and
magazines were filled with amateur (and amateurish)
Chestertonian essays and stories. Chesterton seemed always to know where he wanted to go and how to get there,
and we who admired him wanted to be able to do the same.
It was not that we simply agreed with everything he said—
there was always room for disagreement (at least among
those who did not engage in a cult of Chesterton), and we
were well aware that to agree with everything he said
would be the most blatant disagreement of all with who

he was and what he was. That was the inescapable paradox of agreeing by disagreeing. It was nevertheless true
that we saw quite clearly that, if he did say something, we
could not easily ignore it, that it made great demands on
our thinking, even if that thinking were ultimately to
reject what he said—provided, of course, that our thinking was quite sure it *knew* what he meant, for frequently
there was much more to what he meant than we thought
there was. There was the question, too, of whether he always wanted us to take literally what he said—or seemed
to be saying. All of which brings us to the extremely important matter of his insistence on reason, on rationality,
which for him was comfortable only within the framework
of religious commitment, not in some sort of secular commitment to non-commitment.

Only if we can come to grips with what Chesterton
meant by reason can we make sense of what he meant by
"philosophy," about which he spoke constantly, insisting
that the most important thing about a person, any person, was that person's philosophy, ultimately that person's
view of the cosmos, which in turn has an enormous and
constant influence upon how that person views anything
in the universe. This, finally, tells us a great deal about
what kind of person that person is: "The truth is that a
man's philosophy of the cosmos is directly concerned in
every action of his life."[2] It is in this sense that religious
affirmation was part and parcel of Chesterton's philosophy
of life, and his philosophical reflection was, as he saw it,
a religious response to life.

RESPECT FOR REASON

One of the things that cannot fail to strike anyone who
comes to grips with Chesterton, even in returning to him
many, many years after, is his enormous respect for reason—without, to be sure, idolizing it with the supersti-

tious confidence of the Enlightenment or making on it the impossible demands of Humean scepticism. Among our contemporaries there is scarcely anyone who rings the changes on "reason" as does Chesterton. We cannot always be sure, however, that he means by reason what others mean—even whether he means what we ourselves mean—except insofar as for him it characterizes that which is pre-eminently human in us. One thing is abundantly clear: Chesterton does not mean by reason or rational what a "rationalist" means—even though he sometimes, but rarely, speaks of "rationalism" and "rationalists" in a non-pejorative way, almost as though he forgets the unpleasant things he had previously said of them. Logic is by no means foreign to Chesterton's way of thinking—he has great respect for it and insists upon the need of it, if there is to be rational investigation and discourse—but he refuses to see it as either synonymous or co-terminous with reason. Just as he would never think of confusing individuality and individualism—"Individualism is the death of individuality"[3]—so he would not confuse rationality with rationalism. Perhaps the term that best picks up the meaning he assigns to rationality is "sanity": such that to the term "rational" corresponds the term "sane"—with its overtones of "healthy." By the same token, although he frequently employs the term "reasons" (usually in the plural), he will just as frequently employ the term "grounds," which carries with it the nuances of basis, foundation, solidity, capable of upholding an opinion, either as to how one should think or how one should act. It is quite rational—even "logical"—to follow good reasons, even if, from a purely formal-logical point of view, they are not absolutely compelling. It is not, for example, paradoxical to say, "I have good *reason* (or reasons) to *believe* that what you say is true." Reason, after all, is indispensable, if life is not to be chaotic: "An attempt really to conduct life, without constant reference to reason, would quite certainly break down."[4] To say that reason is indispensable, however, is not to say that it is by itself alone adequate to the conduct of life. In a rather paradoxical way we might say that it is quite rational not to trust reason alone, when it comes to living one's life.

Only if we have a very strong sense of the compossibility of rationality and agnosticism will we escape the mistake of thinking that reason either has or can find all the answers that are to be found, or the mistake of refusing any answer that is not forced on us by rationalistic reason. It might be noted that in this sort of context Chesterton means by "agnosticism" not what we might call the ordinary meaning of the term. For him it means pretty much a willingness to admit non-knowledge, without being paralyzed by it. "Agnosticism . . . is always an admirable thing, so long as it admits that the thing it does not understand may be much superior to the mind which does not understand it."[5] The recognition of this kind of compossibility of rationality and agnosticism is forced on us when, as so frequently happens, rationality takes us as far as it can and still leaves us without strict knowledge or justified rational certainty of what is *beyond* reason. Interestingly enough, it is for Chesterton reason itself that can tell us not to expect reason to take us further than it can, not to expect it to give definitive answers to all the questions it prompts us to ask; it is eminently rational not to trust *only* reason.

In this connection it might be instructive to acknowledge that even Chesterton, like the rest of us, was frequently convinced that reason took him further than in fact it did or was on his side when in fact it was not. To cite but two examples: (1) he had no adequate grounds for judging that he *knew* where *all* the blame for World

War I lay; (2) he did not realize that the Ibsen he disliked (or simply misunderstood) was not the true Ibsen but rather G. B. Shaw's Ibsen. Without going into the question of authority, which belongs to another chapter, we can say that Chesterton was sometimes more certain of the rationality of his views than his reasons gave him the right to be. To say this is not to impugn what he says; it is simply to recognize that it is perfectly reasonable, in the conduct of life, not to look for more certainty than is available; nor, when we say this of Chesterton, need we forget that his adversaries were frequently less justified by reason than he was. In principle Chesterton would vigorously agree that sound reasoning can well tell us to retain a reasonable suspicion that reason alone cannot provide us with definitive answers on many issues, but—moved perhaps by the convert's desire for certainty—he had a tendency to claim rational justification for moral and religious convictions whose rational foundations were not overwhelmingly evident, with regard, for example, to divorce, birth control, pacifism, papal infallibility, women's rights, to mention but a few. It is not inconceivable, of course, that his opinions in these matters were true, but as Plato made clear to us many, many years ago, the truth of an opinion does not change it from opinion to knowledge;[6] only the validity of the arguments for it can do that—and Chesterton's arguments are not always impeccable. One must at least reckon with the possibility that his ingenious mind enabled him to find what he considered rational grounds for affirming what he *preferred* to be true; which is not to throw suspicion on everything he said—we can, after all, use our own reason to evaluate his arguments, and he can both help and encourage us to do precisely this.

Here, however, it is imperative to issue a caution: Chesterton's extraordinary awareness of the inevitability of paradox permitted him for the most part to preserve his balance. There can be no question that he strongly believed in the possibility—however limited it might be—of certain knowledge, without allowing that belief to make him surrender to intolerance. In this connection it might be said that his fondness for paradox and his talent for formulating it preserved him from intolerance; no one knew better than he that a certain opinion is a contradiction in terms, and that opinion, not certainty, is the most constant guide in life. Even after his conversion to the Roman Catholic Church, he never retracted what he had said in 1920: "Now a man preaching what he thinks is a platitude is far more intolerant than a man preaching what he admits is a paradox."[7] When there is paradox, it is rational to be cautious, and unequivocal truth is rare. It is not enough, however, to recognize that opinion is opinion and not certainty; it is also necessary to assert that opinion without solid grounds for holding it is not, properly speaking, opinion at all, it is guesswork, but even solid grounds do not equal a guarantee of truth.

REASON AND PARADOX

Much has been written both for and against Chesterton's admittedly abundant recourse to what is quite erroneously dubbed the "figure of speech" called "paradox." The fact is that truth itself is frequently paradoxical and requires to be stated paradoxically. It is, for example, quite clear that freedom is truly freedom only if it is subject to the constraint of rationality, or that finitude is intelligible only in relation to infinity—and vice versa. Then, of course, there are the paradoxical truths of faith and theology: e.g., Trinity and hypostatic union. It is, of course, arguable that Chesterton overdoes it, that the rapidity with which he summons up paradox after paradox makes it difficult to keep pace with the pyrotechnics of his thought, that he uses rhetorical tricks to obscure the issues of straightforward discussion, that what began as an illuminating manner of speaking and writing gradually became an annoying mannerism, a "mechanical formula." There is no need, I think, to construct elaborate defenses against criticisms such as these; if the critic finds that the proliferation of paradox is tiresome, there is no arguing as to how the critic feels, provided the critic admits that feeling (including feeling "tired") is a subjective state of the critic, which need not be shared by others (it makes no sense to say that someone is tiresome—to anyone but the one who feels tired—no more than it makes sense to say that it is objectively true to say that someone is a bore). As Gilbert and Sullivan have shown us so well—"A paradox, a paradox, a most ingenious paradox" (*Pirates of Penzance*)—in nineteenth-century England paradox had been reduced to an ingenious and fascinating parlor game in which the truth of what was being said was scarcely at issue. Chesterton alludes to this—in the form of a striking paradox—in his 1936 *Autobiography*: "Critics were almost entirely complimentary to what they were pleased to call my brilliant paradoxes; *until* they discovered I really meant what I said."[8] To speak truth in the form of paradox in no way takes away from the truth of what is spoken, nor is it any less rational to speak the truth thus strikingly in the form of paradox than to speak it prosaically; it could, in fact, be more rational. If the enunciation of a truth evokes its opposite in the mind of the reader or hearer, it performs the admirable function of indicating the sense—perhaps the only sense—in which the statement is true. Admittedly, on the other hand, to speak in paradoxes in no way guarantees the truth of what is said. What paradox does is to call attention to what is said, to make it attractive, but leaving it to thinking to judge whether what is said is true.

Unlike those for whom paradox is no more than a fascinating verbal exploit, however, Chesterton seeks to make us puzzle over his meaning, without making us think that there is no meaning. For him the world was a vast battlefield of words and ideas, where the ideas were obviously vastly more important than the words in which they were clothed, but also where the words could be geared to bring the ideas into focus.

Chesterton himself was well aware that frequent recourse to paradox runs the risk of turning it into a rhetorical trick, a risk he did not always succeed in avoiding, but what his use of it showed was not so much cleverness as an extraordinary sensitivity to the omnipresence of mystery, to the seeming contradictions which inevitably accompany existence; he was abundantly endowed with a sense of the sacredness and mystery of all existence—one could call it a "mystical" awareness. That the existence of the universe could not be self-explanatory was, for him, a certainty. To the modern materialist and naturalist mind, of course, mystery (and the mysterious) is anathema. In a sentence that is deliberately as ambiguous as possible—unless one already knows what Chesterton is thinking—he says, "But the modern materialists are not *permitted* to doubt; they are *forbidden* to believe."[9] To be perfectly intelligible—to the materialist—that sentence would have to be re-worded to read: It is not that they are, as are we, permitted to doubt (e.g., the miraculous); they are forbidden to believe what contradicts their dogmatic disbelief. It might be pointed out, incidentally, that by putting the statement the way he did Chesterton accomplished two purposes: (1) he made us think out what his meaning could possibly be; (2) he emphasized that the prohibition to doubt the materialist solution was itself an ungrounded belief, a dogmatic "demand." It might be well to insist here, however, that Chesterton had genuine respect for the sincere atheist, because he was convinced that such an atheist—like Turnbull in *The Ball and the Cross*—really was concerned with truth. Religious belief, after all, is a vocation, a grace, not a demand of natural reason. Chesterton never said it is easy to believe—he himself took a long time working out his beliefs—nor did he ever say that those who do not believe are dishonest; but he quite definitely did say that it makes no sense not to believe, or, perhaps, that there is no way to make sense of existence, if one does not believe, even though there is no "logical" proof that existence *should* make sense. We all know, as we saw earlier, how stupidly annoying the type can be who insists with sham honesty that we simply say exactly what we mean. Not only is it beyond the capacity of language to express exactly what we mean, but it is scarcely possible to employ language consistently without coming up with double meaning. Neville Braybrooke stated this acutely by saying that "For Chesterton paradox, like poetry, was a means of saying several things at the same time."[10] What Braybrooke might have added but did not is that Chesterton was keenly aware that, by not saying several things at one time, one runs the risk that what one does say will be one-sided and, hence, not true. Coming at this from a different angle, Chesterton himself speaks of the impossibility of translating style, because, although the translation may express the meaning of the original, it cannot express its double meaning.[11] We should not forget, however, that what he says of Robert Louis Stevenson is quite applicable to himself: "The author does possess a quite exceptional power of putting what he really means into words that convey it."[12] If we really pay attention, Chesterton's meaning usually comes through.

What it comes down to is that the truths that really count cannot be expressed in a completely unambiguous way, but only in a paradoxical way. Speaking of G. B. Shaw, Chesterton says that "He cannot quite understand life, because he will not accept its contradictions."[13] We might put all this in another way by asking ourselves a question that in the long run forces itself upon us: "Is the universe reasonable (intelligible)?" It should be pointed out, by the way, that the question cannot mean "Do you know it is reasonable?" since there is no conceivable way of knowing that; whether one is materialist or not, one can at best believe it is reasonable. If, however, one means by "reasonable" not paradoxical, it would seem to follow that one must say: "I believe it is not reasonable." The question now becomes, not so much whether one does in fact believe reality to be reasonable, but whether, in a very important sense, it would be irrational to doubt the reasonability of reality, even though it cannot be proved. To put it in a quite Chestertonian way, it is questionable whether one has the right to doubt, if one does not have the courage to doubt the justification of doubting. It is not at all inconceivable that I should have no incontrovertible evidence of the truth of something I believe and that, at the same time, I should be a damned fool if I did not believe it. It clearly makes sense to say that there could be no "science," if scientists did not make an act of faith in the decency of the universe— to which might be added that it would be irrational on the part of the scientist not to make this act of faith. More than that, it would seem, not only is the "decency" of the universe an object of belief, but, to speak with Chesterton, "It is an act of faith to assert that our thoughts have any relation to reality at all,"[14] an act of faith which it would be irrational on the part of the scientist, or of anyone else, not to make; not only is it rational to expect the universe to keep on operating according to the laws that have been governing it, but it would be irrational not to

expect this—nor does expecting it make one a "rationalist." By the same token, however (and Chesterton never
ceased to affirm this), it would be equally irrational to
claim that it could not possibly act in any other way; the
so-called "laws" of nature are not prescriptive but descriptive. Thus, it would be equally irrational to claim that
the "laws" under which our universe operates are the
laws under which any conceivable universe would have
to operate—even though to call it a "universe" is to pre-
suppose that it operates under some set of laws.

It might be well to mention here that, although Chesterton was only minimally acquainted with the mathematics and sciences even of his own day, his attitude was
not anti-scientific; he was simply opposed to science's
making claims it had no right to make. He was unscientific, to be sure, and he betrayed his lack of scientific so-
phistication in many ways. One could go so far as to say
that he gave very little evidence of being adequately ap-
preciative of the significance of scientific endeavor. He
was, however, too intelligent to share the scientific optimism of the nineteenth century, much of which has been
repudiated even by science itself today. Above all, he was
acutely critical of any assumption that science could ar-
rogate to itself the right—or even the capacity—to make
the moral judgments that are essential to authentic human living. There are, it would seem, truths which it
would be insane not to believe, even though there are
no ways of "proving" that they are true. This is where
"sanity" or "healthiness" comes in. "A man of science
isn't trying to prove anything. He's trying to find out
what will prove itself."[15] Chesterton was constant in his
insistence on the universality of moral standards and
principles—sometimes even beyond the bounds of what
rational inquiry can justify. He was, for example, naïve
in his (seeming) conviction that only Euclidean space is

justifiably conceivable or that mathematical axioms and postulates are changeless, but he was far less philosophically unsophisticated than many of his "scientific" contemporaries who believed either that the last word was in on scientific laws or that the last word ever could be in. Nor did he make the mistake of conceiving of "Nature" (which, when spelled with a capital N, as we have already seen, is in truth only a metaphor) as a kind of operator pulling the strings of the universe rather than as a mode of operation which the human mind can justifiably expect to be predictable. The words, clearly, are not Chesterton's, but I feel safe in assuming that he would not reject this attempt to put into words his attitude toward "scientific truth," which I take to be a descriptive formulation of what happens—and can legitimately be expected to happen—without any justification for looking upon it as a prescriptive formulation of what has to happen. The twentieth century, after all, bears eloquent testimony to the corrigibility of many scientific "laws" of the eighteenth and nineteenth centuries.

THE REAL AND THE IDEAL

If there is one thing we cannot do when we speak of Chesterton as a man, as a thinker, as a philosopher, it is to put a label on him and file him away, presumably with others of his kind. Was he an "idealist"? If that means one who constantly emphasizes the primacy of the idea (ideal, exemplar) over its exemplification in the concrete world of particulars, no one of which measures up to the idea, the answer has to be yes. If it means one whose feet were not always firmly planted in the homely—and homey—solidity of material reality, the answer is a resounding no. Was he, then, a "realist"? In the sense that he considered reality—including but not exclusively material reality—as really real, yes. In the sense that material reality is real without any reference to mind as its source, a very strong no. In a very significant sense, however, it is important to recognize that questions such as these in relation to Chesterton are simply foolish. There is no way of classifying his thought as any kind of "ism." Perhaps the question that should be asked is whether Chesterton's thinking linked him to any "school," either by membership in or resemblance to an identifiable way of thinking. Here, too, the question is a misguided one. Among the renowned philosophers in history Chesterton had a very high regard for Plato, for Aristotle, and for Thomas Aquinas. To the extent that he even knew Plato, any relation to Plato can be limited to the significant conviction that the basic idea of which any particular reality is the copy is more real than the copy of it is. This did not prevent him from frequently misinterpreting Plato by taking him too literally. His familiarity with Aristotle, too, was at best passing. He was strongly impressed—and rightly so— by Aristotle's "common sense." He also saw in him perhaps the most important molder of Western thinking, but his knowledge of Aristotle remained superficial. Even with regard to Thomas Aquinas, whom he knew best— well enough, as we have noted, to write one of the most brilliant monographs written about Aquinas' thought— he was not of the "Thomistic" school in any significant sense (despite what the "Thomist" admirers of Chesterton would like him to be). What Chesterton found—and this says a great deal for the profundity of his own thinking—was that, when he had thought his way through to a highly metaphysical view of the totality of reality, that view turned out to resemble in highly significant ways that of Aquinas. Whether we can call this the "influence" of Aquinas is difficult to say. What is most striking, however, is not the degree to which Chesterton's thinking resembles or is influenced by the thought of others, but the manner in which he can express the profoundist thought in the fewest possible words—how he can make the reader want what he says to be true, without, for the most part, descending to mere rhetorical presentations; he is not merely persuasive, he is convincing.

Like everyone else, Chesterton slipped once in a while, but he never renounced his basic conviction that language is essentially in the service of thought, and that mere stylistic or rhetorical brillance always carries with it the risk of reversing this relationship. Here it is that, once more, his abundant use of paradox comes in. One can, it is true, become bored with or surfeited by Chesterton's paradoxes; rarely can one say that they fail to do their job or that they are not significant ways of saying what needs to be said. We need but remind ourselves that the point of paradox is not being clever but rather getting a point across effectively, making us sit up and take notice. Maisie Ward makes the right point very clearly: "I think," she says, "nearly all his paradoxes were either the startling expression of an entirely neglected truth, or the startling re-emphasis of the neglected side of a truth."[16] His treasury of one-liners is inexhaustible: one wonders whether they are often intended not so much to convey thought as to stimulate it. "The use of paradox," he says, "is to awaken the mind"[17] or, as we ourselves might say, to jolt the mind into a recognition of the truth. Speaking of George Eliot, he calls her "an irrational rationalist, because she asked for arduous sacrifice, for asceticism, without any reason for it."[18] The "Romantics" too he convicts of intellectual inconsistency: they "rushed back to medieval art and never even noticed medieval philosophy,"[19] thus failing to see that neither the art nor the philosophy is intelligible if we focus on the one without the other. In *Orthodoxy* (much earlier in his career but almost prophetic in character), he comes out with one of the most succinct yet pregnant paradoxes of all, which he will repeat in one form or another over and over again. He speaks of "the liberty to bind oneself,"[20] a most effective form of liberty, precisely as a manifestation of responsible choice, the choice to be responsible.

In the face of the English tendency to equate rationality and logicality, Chesterton insists on the place of imagination in philosophy (as in science, although he scarcely seems to recognize the implications of the latter)—a kind of "imaginative reason" of which "enthusiasm" is a rational stance: "You can only find truth with logic if you have already found truth without it."[21] One might, of course, question whether logic is geared to "find" truth at all. Another way of putting pretty much the same thing is found in his book on G. B. Shaw: "It is better to speak wisdom foolishly, like the saints, rather than to speak folly wisely, like the Dons."[22] He never tired of burlesquing the stuffy wisdom of the "intelligentsia." Hugh Kenner says of Chesterton that "He made men see what they had not seen before. He made them know."[23] One might ask, perhaps, if he did not make them see that they had already seen without realizing it. Frequently, Chesterton was accused of being a dogmatist—in itself a quite dogmatic accusation—which he quite cheerfully admitted to be true, since it is quite normal to be convinced that what one believes to be true is in fact true. "The dogmatist is interested only in the truth, and only in the truth because it is true."[24] (It might be worth noting that he frequently employs the adverb "only" in an ambiguous and possibly misleading way.) In short, we are all dogmatists, even those of us who are dogmatic anti-dogmatists. Of Dickens, for example, Chesterton writes: "He had, for instance, that dislike of defined dogmas, which really means a preference for unexamined dogmas."[25] This last, of course, is, more often than not, a means of avoiding what, for emotional reasons, one does not like. "When you meet a modern man, he is always coming from a place, not going to it."[26] In addition, such a "modern" tends to be wrapped up in language rather than in thought: "What is the matter with the curious cultural atmosphere around us is that it abounds, not in trains of thought, but in tags of language."[27] There is no need at all to deny that a fair amount of what Chesterton wrote could be justifiably classed as "ephemeral journalism" (no one who wrote enough to fill 93 volumes could fail to write some of that), so long as we recognize that the thinking behind the writing was not ephemeral at all. One reason why Chesterton is still so readable today is that he is constantly concerned with issues that do not cease to be issues.

In my opinion it is highly rational, as I have already said, to hold strongly opinions one has solid reasons to believe are true. There are, however, a number of provisos that must be attached to a statement like that, or even to an attitude like that. The first of these is that we recognize that an opinion is an opinion, not a certainty, and that any belief is, strictly speaking, an opinion, even though the reason for holding it may be supernatural rather than natural. Here we must be quick to admit that Chesterton—like many converts of his day—was not above thinking he had more certainty than he did have regarding some of his opinions. He was not, however, a bigot—understanding bigotry, as he himself did, as "the incapacity to conceive seriously an alternative to a proposition."[28] On the other hand, he saw no reason to change an opinion until the reasons for holding it had ceased to be adequate or, to put the same thing positively, reasons for changing his opinion had convinced him to do so. Nor would he ever admit that the multiplication of opinions is any argument whatever for claiming that none of them is true. By the same token, if we are convinced that we see the truth of a position—assuming that seeing makes sense in the context—there is no reason to fear the opposition's claim that seeing is not a rational ground for firm affirmation or assent, so long as we are at the same time willing to admit that seeing is not to be confused with connected argument. Nor should we be unwilling to admit that "instinctive wisdom" can and sometimes should supplant strictly logical deduction—which, if based on false premises, proves nothing at all.

This, however, introduces another proviso that is difficult to formulate. Granted that having good reasons either to hold or to change an opinion justifies holding or changing it, just what is it that permits us to recognize reasons as "good"? It might be that we answer in Chestertonian fashion that a rationality which keeps in touch with the reality it reasons about is reliable (or reasonable) rationality, but this sort of thing runs the risk of being, if not circular, at least spiral. It would seem that Chesterton is—along with Aristotle and Thomas Aquinas, incidentally—holding that at least first principles are certain, in the sense that they reveal themselves to sound thinking as indisputable, that they are in an intelligible sense "self-evident." Consistent faithfulness to first principles, then, would ensure the validity of the affirmations flowing from them. Still, if I interpret him correctly, what Chesterton is saying is not that we *infer* divers conclusions from first principles—that would indeed involve circularity—but that what rational thinking "sees" as imposing itself can stand trial at the bar of first principles, and, if not found wanting, can be justifiably assented to. I am, of course, by no means sure that Chesterton would say it this way (he would undoubtedly say it more arrestingly), but I do feel that this is a fairly faithful analysis of the movement of his thinking—provided, of course, that we see in Chesterton what can be called the "instinctive rationality" I spoke of above, particularly in the approach to moral and psychological problems. This, of course, demands extreme caution in approaching Chesterton's thought analytically at all. His thinking is almost always on the borderline of the mystical, and sometimes it crosses that line. Here it is that we must take seriously Dale's insistence that Chesterton "comes across as . . . a cross between a prophet and a clown who willingly plays the fool to make his point";[29] to which we might add Maisie Ward's characterization of his "inspired fooling."[30] Frequently, when Chesterton is fooling most riotously he is at his most profound—and most serious.

This last, of course, brings up a question which we may not be able to answer, since Chesterton himself did not explicitly answer it: Was Chesterton's manner of writing—and speaking—with its amazing blend of jest and seriousness, determined by the audience he had in view, or did he by his own manner mold an audience that would respond predictably to his kind of "inspired fooling"? One thing is abundantly clear: only by frequent recourse to paradoxical expression could he open the eyes and the minds of his audience to both the striking character and the calm assurance of the positions he was proclaiming. It is precisely because what he says is frequently not wholly true that it has the power to evoke in an audience a thinking adequate to the matter in hand, out of which emerges a firm grasp of *well-grounded* truth. Chesterton himself illustrates what I mean here by referring to a statement of Stevenson, whose true meaning comes through only when all its possible false meanings have been eliminated. Chesterton quotes Stevenson as saying: "To travel hopefully is better than to arrive."[31] Only after he has shown that the statement "gives a loophole for every sort of sophistry and unreason" can he then draw the conclusion that truly counts: "It is one thing to travel hopefully, and say half in jest that it is better than to arrive. It is another thing to travel hopelessly, because you know you will never arrive."[32] To write like this, obviously, is to run the risk that one's readers will be so impressed by the cleverness of the expression that they will miss the precise point one is trying to make. On the other hand, one runs the risk of totally missing the point of religious or moral truth, if one seeks to express it unparadoxically. Imagine trying to remove every paradoxical statement from the New Testament!

REASON AND ENTHUSIASM

In Chesterton's Edwardian world there was a spirit abroad according to which being rational was equated with being prosaic. That spirit, of course, has not been completely laid to rest even today, but it is possible for us to miss his gargantuan efforts to do battle with that spirit in his own day, because the issue is for us not nearly so burning as it was for Chesterton. If one takes seriously the equating of the rational and the prosaic, one would seem to be left with but two options: either one chooses to be rational, thus draining life of both mystery and color, or one chooses poetry, excitement, the magic of real living, and the challenge of freedom, thus forgoing the level-headedness of monotony—or, perhaps, the monotony of level-headedness. But, there is in fact a third option: without necessarily becoming a Chesterton one can see that the rational and the mystical need not be mutually exclusive, that truth is not limited to what can be proved with impeccable logic, that there is more to thinking than what can be programmed into a computer. This might take the form of a far higher regard for the traditions which a plodding logic cannot fathom, without descending to the acceptance of each passing fancy as it sky-rockets across the horizon. Above all, the reconciliation of the rational and the poetic will make us more aware that words are no substitutes for thought, that labels do not enable us to dispense with meanings, that rational discourse need not inevitably be dull. Nor, in all of this, need we be lulled into the opposite mistake of devaluating rationality—connected argumentation in the quest for truth. By the same token, we shall be missing Chesterton's thought altogether if we fail to see that there is meaning only where there is thinking; there is value only where there is willing.

Now, none of this will make any sense whatsoever, unless correct thinking involves some sort of correspondence of the mind with the objective reality of what it thinks, nor will correct willing make sense unless it corresponds with the objective value of what is willed. One might go so far as to say that the backbone of all Chesterton's philosophical thinking, religious conviction, and moral judgment is to be found right there. It is not inconceivable, of course, that some might find it tiring that Chesterton repeats this sort of thing over and over again in all sorts of forms, but the answer to that is that repetition is necessary, precisely because truth cannot ever be adequately said and, therefore, must be said again and again, nor can any one way of saying it be adequate to the truth that requires to be said. Being convinced that what one thinks is true is in fact true is not incompatible with its not being true, but it is incompatible with a belief either that there is no truth or that truth is unattainable, that one can search for the truth but one cannot find it, or that one never has the right to think that what one has found is in fact truth. There is simply no need that all philosophical propositions be only hypothetical. There is, however, a need to recognize that the quest for truth does not make sense, if we do not see that the quest for truth and the quest for God are inseparable. There can be no question that, in Chesterton's view, to seek truth is to seek God, even though the seeker may not be aware of this, and that to find truth is to find God, even though, as in his own case, the implications of that finding may be long in coming through, even if, indeed, they never quite succeed in getting through. If, in fact, this truth *did* get through to Chesterton, then, presumably, it did not get through to, for example, Shaw and Wells—and there is no reason to claim that they were not honest seekers; at least Chesterton never said that. Perhaps they were simply not adequately rational.

Here it is that Chesterton comes across as the quintessential Christian apologete, foreshadowed in his writing before his becoming a Christian and long before his conversion to Roman Catholicism. What is most striking, however, is his unalterable conviction that both the voyage *to* faith and the voyage *in* faith are part and parcel of an intellectual venture, not of an emotional "trip"— remembering, of course, that intellectual conviction unaccompanied by emotional exhilaration is for Chesterton simply inconceivable. He was not only a seeker *after* truth but also, and perhaps more significantly, an enthusiast *about* the truth, as that which satisfies the deepest cravings of the human spirit. "We have got to make them see that conversion is the beginning of an active, fruitful, progressive and even adventurous life of the intellect"[33]— we might add, a most enjoyable life, at that! Once more we have the Chestertonian emphasis on rationality, not that Chesterton would ever make the mistake of identifying faith and rationality, but he would unceasingly insist on their compatibility, on the rational satisfaction to be found in faith, or perhaps, if we wish to employ the medieval distinction between *intellectus* and *ratio*, on the intellectual satisfaction that faith affords. That which, more than anything else, characterizes the human, precisely as human, is reason—contra Rousseau, Emerson, et al.—but it is rational *not* to rely on reason alone in the conduct of life. Here it might well be asked whether Chesterton, despite the fact that he scarcely knew Hegel—and disliked the little he did know—was not in his own way acknowledging the Hegelian concept of "objective rationality," i.e., the rationality of a content of thought which has not been arrived at by exclusively rational processes but which can be seen, after having been affirmed, as quite clearly reasonable, even compelling. This sort of thing can seem to be coming perilously close to what we call "rationalizing," which has to do primarily with a mode of thinking that follows upon a mode of acting, seeking to justify the acting by finding reasons to legitimize it, when in fact such reasons either were not antecedently operative or not antecedently thought out. There is, however, a great difference, and neither Hegel nor Chesterton is speaking of this sort of rationalizing. With neither is it a question of subsequently *inventing* reasons to justify an antecedent mode of behavior; rather it is a question, primarily in the area of religious conviction, of recognizing that religious truths (mysteries), which have been affirmed not as the result of a rational process of discovery, turn out to be not only intellectually acceptable but even compelling.

It is most interesting, incidentally, that, without the one thinker influencing the other, both Chesterton and Hegel give as examples of this the "paradoxical" truths of a triplicity of persons in one God, God becoming incarnate in a human individual, and the divine Spirit dwelling in a human community. Neither says that human reason could *discover* these truths; both say that we can quite reasonably believe them. Chesterton goes so far as to claim that there is a certain "common sense" acceptability in these paradoxical truths.[34] It may, for example, be true that there are no compelling "proofs" for the existence of God—no more than there are compelling proofs for the existence of my neighbor. It may even be that experience is more compelling in requiring me to believe in the existence of my neighbor. But it is rather doubtful that one can believe in the reality of Nature—which is not a machine—and not believe in the reality of God. It might be added that only with great difficulty *can* one believe in a Nature that is equivalently a machine. "Poets, even Pagans, can only directly believe in Nature if they indirectly believe in God."[35] No one has any trouble accepting that the product of human art is neither self-producing nor self-supporting. From that it is no giant step to understanding that the same is true of nature; it is neither its own source nor its own support. At the risk of becoming otiose it might not be without interest to note that both Hegel and Chesterton, each in his own age, was concerned to defend the primacy of ideas in an age that was turning toward an affirmation of the primacy of matter. Both had a profound conviction of the distinction between nature and spirit, such that they could immediately see the fatuousness of merely doing what comes naturally; the human, after all, is *not* simply a being of nature, which means, of course, that the evil which humans bring into the world is not simply part and parcel of the natural order; it is chosen by the supremely spiritual activity of willing; without spirit there is no evil. By the same token, it must be said that the contention that the only acceptable explanation of the way things are has to be found in nature simply makes no sense. Both Hegel and Chesterton were aware of the need to blend the natural and the supernatural. If the world is rational, and it would seem that it must be if there is to be any knowledge of it at all, then its rationality has its source—and not merely its articulation—in mind, in the only mind that could possibly be, its source, infinite mind. It is certainly no more rational to disbelieve this than to believe it. Perhaps what needs to be said is that the "dialectical" method of Hegel and the "paradoxical" method of Chesterton have more than a little in common—they both saw that reality itself dictated the method.

THE MEANING OF BELIEF

To speak in this way about "believing" is not necessarily to speak of religious belief. There are any number of things we believe without being able to prove, which, in fact, it would be insane not to believe. Early in his career Chesterton put this in a very challenging way, which, interestingly enough, contains strong echoes of David Hume:

> Leave religion for the moment wholly out of the question. All sane men, I say, believe firmly and unalterably in a certain number of things which are unproved and unprovable. Let us state them roughly.
>
> (1) Every sane man believes that the world around him and the people in it are real, and not his own delusion or dream. No man starts burning London in the belief that his servant will soon wake him for breakfast. But that I, at any given moment, am not in a dream, is unproved and unprovable. That anything exists except myself is unproved and unprovable.
>
> (2) All sane men believe that this world not only exists, but matters. Every man believes there is a sort of obligation on us to interest ourselves in this vision or panorama of life. He would think a man wrong who said, "I did not ask for this farce and it bores me. I am aware that an old lady is being murdered downstairs, but I am going to sleep." That there is any such duty to improve the things we did not make is a thing unproved and unprovable.
>
> (3) All sane men believe that there is such a thing as a self or ego, which is continuous. There is no inch of my brain

matter the same as it was ten years ago. But if I have saved a man in battle ten years ago, I am proud; if I have run away, I am ashamed. That there is such a paramount "I" is unproved and unprovable. But it is more than unproved and unprovable; it is definitely disputed by many meta-physicians.

(4) Lastly, most sane men believe, and all sane men in prac-tice assume, that they have a power of choice and responsi-bility for action. . . .[36]

It is well to insist again, by the way, that "unproved and unprovable" are not synonymous with "unknown and un-knowable." Technically speaking, knowing and believing are not the same, but it can make a great deal of good sense to say "I *know* that it is reasonable to *believe* the things Chesterton speaks of here." In this connection Hil-aire Belloc refers to Chesterton's attitude as eminently "philosophical": "I use the word 'philosophical' here to mean the search for truth in the reasonable hope of attain-ing it."[37] It might be well to add that the truth Chesterton reasonably hoped to attain was presumably truth about human living: moral truth, religious truth, social and po-litical truth.

This preliminary sketch of Chesterton the rational in-quirer would be woefully incomplete did it not give us some sort of glimpse into how he related to others, not merely intellectually but, perhaps more significantly, per-sonally. Much of this can be gained simply by reflecting on the enthusiasm with which he encountered life and the way he inevitably shared his enthusiasm for the life he encountered. It is impossible to read what he wrote without gradually forming a rather accurate picture of him as a person, as one who cared very much not only for truth but also that fellow human beings should have the opportunity to think truly and to think for them-selves. We are fortunate, however, to have not only his books and articles, his poems and stories, his literary criticism, and serious apologetics, from which to come to know him as the source of all this; we also have the recollections of those contemporaries who knew him well: his brother Cecil, his close friends Belloc, Titterton, Father O'Connor, Maisie Ward, and, perhaps his oldest friend, E. C. Bentley. We also have the scattered recollections gathered by Cyril Clemens and Maisie Ward, which reveal to us how he came across as a person to those who had contact with him over the years. Without going into the many testimonies regarding his kindness, his love of children, his generosity, patience, humor, we have the many memories of his brilliant gift for conversation—out of which, it would seem, his writing flowed—his passionate love of debate, his tenacity in not letting an argument be put to sleep, his authentic respect for those with whom he disagreed. There is one particular characteristic, however, that stands out both in Cyril Clemens' 1939 book, *Chesterton as Seen by His Contemporaries*, and in Maisie Ward's *Return to Chesterton* (1952): a very special gift he had for making others feel that they were interesting and intelligent. Maisie Ward in her biography, for example, emphasizes the ease with which he could make anyone feel that he or she was making a contribution to the flow of ideas in conversation:

> Even more attractive to most of us was his fashion of making us feel that we contributed something very worthwhile. He would take something one had said and develop it till it shone and glowed, not from its own worth but from what he made of it. Almost everything could thus become a starting point for a train of his best thought. And the style disliked by some in his writings was so completely the man himself that it was the same in conversation as in his books. He would approach a topic from every side throwing light on those contradictory elements that made a paradox.[38]

Apparently Chesterton was incapable of finding anyone uninteresting or a bore. The responsibility, it would
seem, for anyone being a bore lay with the one who found
him or her boring. Maisie Ward quotes an unnamed man
friend as saying, "When you talked with Chesterton you
didn't feel how brilliant he was but how brilliant you
were."[39] Even allowing for the rather obvious exaggeration here, Chesterton comes across, not as one who made
an effort to help people find themselves interesting, but as
one who himself actually found them interesting. It was
because he found people intelligent and interesting that
they could find themselves so. In any event, the picture
that comes through is of one who found life so interesting that he could not find people uninteresting. He undoubtedly saw in them more than was there, but it is also
undoubtedly true that, when they were with him, there
was more in them than there usually was. The point is
that (and this leads us into the next chapter) Chesterton
did in fact find the world and the people in it wonderfully
exciting—which is to say *real*: "It is, in short, the man who
thinks ordinary things common who is really the man
who is living in an unreal world."[40]

3

In Quest of Value

WE HAVE ALREADY SEEN how Chesterton's contemporaries and those who were closest to him experienced him as a person, a person who was just plain good. It was almost as though he did not have to work at being good, as though goodness was like an aura that clung about him. It might be more accurate to say, however, that he had an orientation—not merely natural but acquired by much exercise—to what was worthwhile, accompanied by an acute realization that nothing is more worthwhile than being a worthwhile person, one who consistently contributes to the well-being of those around him. It might seem that this sort of language is descriptive of an "optimist," but Chesterton did not want to be classified with the "optimists," despite the fact that he was the sworn enemy of all forms of pessimism. As he saw it, "optimist" was a designation for one who was "rationally" convinced that the world in which we live is the best possible world—which, of course, the pessimist could readily accept, since the only possible world for the pessimist is one that is not good at all. What characterized Chesterton was his ability to see whatever is as originally good (we might call it "unspoiled")—good simply because it is and comes from the hand of God. There is moral evil in the world, to be sure, lots of it, but it is there because it has been introduced into the world by the free activity of spiritual beings.

Here it is necessary to make a very careful distinction—which Chesterton himself did not always make too clearly—between "bad" and "evil," particularly as adjectives, a distinction not too different from the Scholastic distinction between "physical" and "moral" evil, where "evil" is a noun, and also a distinction which Chesterton does not trouble to articulate. One can speak of an instrument—say, a gun, a sword, a bomb—as "bad," in the sense that it does not perform its intended function well; one cannot call it "evil." The only evil one can speak of here is the evil use someone puts it to—the evil intent of the user.[1] On the other hand, there is never any question in Chesterton's thought of an unthinking canonization of the natural, but there quite definitely is a recognition that evil is not part and parcel of nature, even though imperfection is; if evil is to exist at all it has to be introduced by beings who are more than merely natural, beings who alone can in the moral sense be either good or evil, precisely because they can both know and freely will. By the same token, however, it should be added that only spiritual beings can appreciate the worthwhileness of things. This, in turn, carries with it the risk that people of good will will work so hard to bring about what is good (worthwhile) that the working becomes more important than what they work for.[2] This is a constant in Chesterton's thinking, the distinction between ends and means, where the end is always prior to the means, in the sense both that the end is more important than the means and that it must be intended before the means are intended— the cart is always before the horse. "All these silly words like Service and Efficiency and Practicality and the rest fail because they worship the means and not the end."[3] The activity of producing is never more important than the product; still less important is the profit made as the result of the producing—a practical conclusion Chesterton never tired of drawing, without, of course, supporting the vicious form of the conclusion that the goodness of the end sanctifies the use of evil means.

If, however, we follow too closely Chesterton's views on the unspoiledness of natural things, finding evil only in what spiritual beings do with or to the natural, we run the risk of failing to see that it is the vocation of human beings, by their activity, to improve what is found in nature—e.g., improving its productivity in order to support life, harnessing its power in order to make life more livable, or exploiting its medicinal capacities in order to prolong life. This is not to say that Chesterton in any way failed to see that it is always life that is the end of the activities ordered to it; he simply does not stress the productive kind of activity that uses nature to improve life. It must be admitted, however, that he does have a kind of distrust of machinery and not only the capitalist ownership but also the labor-saving character thereof—and the manner in which it turns humans into machines. Still, one thing is certain: Chesterton never ceases to insist that life is good, life is worthwhile—no matter how much suffering it may entail, no matter how many pessimists may be hiding in the wings to proclaim how bad it is. In this connection it is interesting to note that, although he considers both the question and the answer to the matter of whether life is good to be philosophical, he does not look upon them as reserved to professional philosophers, especially those of his own day, who had shown themselves singularly incompetent in dealing with questions of value. In an encomium of George Bernard Shaw he says:

> He has stood up for the fact that philosophy is not the concern of those who pass through Divinity and Greats, but of those who pass through birth and death. . . . Only the mass of men, for instance, have authority to say whether life is good. Whether life is good is an especially mystical and delicate question, and, like all such questions, is asked in words of one syllable. It is also answered in words of one syllable; and Bernard Shaw (as also mankind) answers "yes."[4]

It might be tempting to look upon philosophy as a specialized discipline that is under the control of an establishment made up of those who have secured a doctoral degree, preferably at a prestigious Anglo-Saxon university. Neither Shaw nor Chesterton, no matter how violently they might disagree on everything else, could accept this kind of segregation.

PHILOSOPHY AND TRUTH

Here it is that we must look once more, however briefly, at what Chesterton considers philosophy in fact to be. Strictly speaking, he never provides us with a definition of philosophy, for the rather simple reason that no linguistic formula will ever be able to capture the inexhaustible richness of the reality of it. It is, however, possible—and legitimate—to speak of one's "philosophy" as the sum-total of what one holds to be both indubitably true and important, if one's life is to be meaningful. It may of course seem that in speaking the way I do about philosophy I am either hedging or verging on scepticism if in treating of "philosophy" I do not introduce the concept of *knowing*. The reason for this, however, is simple enough—knowing is far more difficult to pin down than is philosophy. If what one means by "knowing" is what David Hume means, then the only knowing there is is trivial, and that gets us nowhere. If one means what Immanuel Kant means by knowing, then all we can know is how we must experience reality, not whether reality *is* the way we *experience* it. Then again, one might mean by knowing what Hegel means, claiming as he does that it characterizes philosophy in the only significant sense of that term and involves a dialectical relationship between the knower and the known, but that would entail understanding Hegel's *Phenomenology of Spirit*, which no one finds easy to do, and scarcely anyone finds particularly inviting to try (although I am convinced that Chesterton would have found it quite congenial, had he ever had occasion to read it in other than the only English translation available to him in his day). Perhaps the best we can do is to describe Chesterton's philosophy as the set of positions he held based on very solid reasons which he had thought out very carefully. This, of course, puts us in the possibly uncomfortable position of trying to determine what constitutes a "solid" reason. One answer to that question is that a good reason for considering a position to be true is the fact that ordinary human beings consistently consider it to be true—which inevitably involves considering also to be true whatever is necessarily implied by the position in question. This, then, brings us back to Chesterton's four typical certainties which we saw enunciated at the end of Chapter 2, and which he considered it "insane" (in the sense of *unsound* or *unhealthy*) to doubt.

There is a subtle sense in which Chesterton was quite convinced that he was right about a good number of things, a conviction that led many of his adversaries—and even some of his sympathizers—to consider him dogmatic. He himself, however, was the first to admit that he was dogmatic, as is anyone else who holds anything to be indubitably true. The big difference is precisely that he admitted being dogmatic, whereas those who held that he was indubitably wrong did not even recognize their own dogmas as dogmas. It might be well to point out here that, for Chesterton, "indubitably true" meant something like "what I have no good reason to consider not true," whereas, for his adversaries "indubitably wrong" means more like "what I simply *know* to be wrong." In this connection we might try to understand his use of the expression "The Catholic Philosophy"[5] as simply the view of reality and life which he finds congenial to his life-long intellectual quest—which intellectual quest had led him to the Catholic Church. This, of course, becomes particularly important where what is in question is the morally right, the right thing to do. It may very well be, of course, that certainty in moral matters is frequently difficult to achieve, but it is simply irrational to have no convictions at all as to what is right and what is wrong to do, or, worse still, to have very strong convictions that it is wrong to have these kinds of convictions. Nor need it strain the mind greatly to recognize that what is right is what is to be done, and what is wrong is what is to be avoided, even though the doing or avoiding may demand considerable courage. The axiom "good is to be done, evil is to be avoided" (*bonum est faciendum*; *malum est vitandum*) is not, incidentally, a tautology, it is simply a definition of what we *mean* by "good" and "evil." It may even take courage to be assured that what I think is right is right and what I think is wrong is wrong, but if I have no such convictions I am worth very little. Here it is that Chesterton insists we can and must be certain we are right, in the sense of having no reasonable doubt; or else we cannot fight for what is right and against what is wrong—we can only say that "right" and "wrong" are meaningless.[6]

What enables us to distinguish between the right and the wrong—not merely in the abstract—according to Chesterton, is "common sense," or what we might call, in the language of Aristotle, "practical wisdom." Chestertonian "common sense" could be called a parade example of the paradoxical; it is a knowing that is at the same time a non-knowing, because it carries with it no guarantee of its own infallibility and at the same time issues a reasonable demand for acceptance and compliance. One is reminded of Socrates' paradoxical claim that all he knew was that he did not know, and yet that he did know one thing: namely, that what he was doing was the right thing to do—i.e., asking all the questions he asked with the reasonable conviction that true answers to those questions were attainable. It might be answered that, although Socrates (or Plato) never really formulated those answers, we who read Plato's dialogues imperceptibly discover that the answers have been revealed to us, and that we can justifiably take these answers as guides to action. It is in this sense, too, that we must interpret Chesterton's paradoxical claim: if we follow carefully what he says, we can make our own decision as to whether or not we accept it as true.

It is interesting in this connection that Chesterton never tires of finding in traditional fairy tales the foundations of moral goodness and moral judgment.[7] The world of the fairies is a world of important values, where each tale is a lesson in goodness, each portrays the eventual triumph of good over evil.[8] This, however, does not mean that he was naïvely unaware of the existence of evil in the real world. No one was more aware of the reality of evil in the world than was G. K. C., but, with the paradoxical twist that so characterized not only his thought but also his experiences, it was, in the words of Christopher Hollis, "the existence of evil which first led him to the appreciation of goodness."[9] In this sense we have to call Chesterton an optimist, just as he called Hamlet an optimist—i.e., one who in the very midst of human evil finds more good than evil. "Many fine optimists have praised man when they feel like praising him. Only Hamlet has praised man when he felt like kicking him as a monkey of the mud. Many poets, like Shelley and Whitman, have been optimistic when they felt optimistic. Only Shakespeare has been optimistic when he felt pessimistic."[10] Chesterton was every inch a realist and, thus, could not find the world in which we live satisfactory. As he saw it, to be content with the way things are in the world is to live in an unreal world.[11] There can be no question that Chesterton did address himself to the problem of evil in a world which is created good by God. He did not, however, do so in abstract terms. It is almost as though he had discovered the doctrine of the Fall by thinking it out for himself: there is evil in a good world because human beings have the capacity to misuse their divinely-given freedom. Thus, he saw very clearly that the evil of the Fall offered no argument against the goodness of creation—or of the Creator.[12] In this connection Chesterton was quick to see how important it is to recognize the evil in ourselves. We must be very much aware that nature in itself is never malign but that human beings only too often can be and are; both good and evil, after all, reside in spirit. He was, nevertheless, convinced that virtue—abundance of it—is to be found in this world of ours.[13] It makes no sense, of course, to speak of good and evil, in quantitative terms, as though there could be "more" of one than of the other in our world, but if one is determined, as was Chesterton, to look for good in the world, one will find it.[14] Precisely because this is true, however, there remains one mystery about Chesterton which I have never been able to solve, nor have I been able to find anyone who has solved it (or, for that matter, even treated it). Even though he has some harsh things to say about any number of authors—e.g., Shelley, Swinburne, Byron, Hardy, etc.—he always, with one exception, can find something good to say. That one exception is Erich Maria Remarque, whom he calls "that dirty, snivelling pacifist," regarding him, it would seem, as the very quintessence of evil.[15] The mystery in this case does not consist in *how* he felt about Remarque—everyone can make a mistake—but in *why* he felt the way he did. He never tells us why, and his commentators are uniformly silent on the question. For the most part Chesterton trusts the judgment of "ordinary" people, most of whom, I venture to say, would agree that *All Quiet on the Western Front* is one of the truly great novels of the twentieth century. Not so Chesterton. Why? One can only guess. (1) There was a lingering prudishness about Chesterton that made him resent Remarque's explicit treatment of sex. But Remarque is not nearly so explicitly sensual in this as are Somerset Maugham or D. H. Lawrence, and Chesterton does not complain of these authors (at least he finds some good in them). (2) Chesterton hated "pacifists" with a passion, but his own views on war were thoroughly unrealistic, and Remarque simply was not a doctrinaire pacifist—neither was he a Prussian militarist; he simply suffered through a very cruel war which he had not started. It has been said, with a great deal of truth, that Remarque never really grew up—but that has been said of Chesterton, too.

CHESTERTONIAN LOVE

If we leave aside, then, this strange exception, we can say of Chesterton what he himself said of Robert Browning: "He did not love humanity but men. His sense of the difference between one man and another would have made the thought of melting them into a lump called humanity simply loathsome and prosaic."[16] Like Browning, Chesterton was able to see the divinity in the faces of people he met on the street. To be able to do that demands a clarity of vision that sees at once the reality of sin and the lovableness of the sinner. Once again, of course, it is easy enough in the abstract to separate the sinner from the sin, but when we are faced with the concrete reality of the sinner sinning, it is not really so easy to be forgiving.[17] If we insist on being rational and rational only, it is impossible[18]—perhaps the only "reason" we can have for loving our enemies is that Jesus Christ told us to, without our ever quite knowing why he did; only saints, like Francis, did. On the other hand our attitude toward people will be governed to a great extent by what we are interested in and looking for in them. If we are convinced that there are more virtues than vices in the people we meet, the more likely we are to find virtues than vices. "We ought to be interested in that darkest and most real part of a man in which dwell not the vices that he does not display, but the virtues that he cannot."[19]

It is not too easy to know exactly what Chesterton means by the virtues one "cannot" display, but his constant insistence on the difference between subjection to moral law, as opposed to subjection to social pressure, which are in inverse proportion to each other, would seem to indicate that social pressure can all too readily cause us to keep the truly good in us hidden, a view that contains a subtle critique of Victorian (and Edwardian) Britain. "The fear is that as morals become less urgent, manners will become more so; and men who have forgotten the fear of God will retain the fear of Littimer."[20] Where, on the other hand, the balance is a healthier one, the emergence of evil will always come as a surprise, as unexpected. If what we expect is the good, the evil will always be a surprise—and we shall want to do something about it.[21] It might be worthwhile to note here that where there is question of strong beliefs we all, like Chesterton, have a tendency to overstate our case. It would be a mistake, however, to think that he was so naïve as not to know that the battle with evil is unending and without compromise; that there is no definitive victory in this life.

Despite the fact that Chesterton is often very critical of the Victorians, precisely because of their extraordinary respect for respectability, letting it take the place of both religion and morality, there is still a sense in which he himself is a product of the Victorian age. This is not to say that he was a typical Victorian, sharing the very faiths he criticized. Strictly speaking he was an Edwardian, but that is not to the point here. What is to the point is that he so well understood the Victorians: not merely their literature, which he understood perhaps better than anyone of his own generation, but also their whole way of life, which had such an effect on the English way of life up to World War I—and even, to some extent, up to World War II. "Thus, they thought that respectability would last longer than religion; and by assuming that respectability and morality could exist outside the individual, they paid more attention to discussing it than to practising it."[22] Chesterton was only too well aware that the stability of such a society could not long outlive the departure of the strong support of religion and morality, and one can understand from this that his emphasis on both religion and morality became more and more pronounced as time went on. Still there was one conviction characteristic of the Victorian age that stayed with Chesterton and did much to form his way of life. "Like Matthew Arnold, the last and most sceptical of them, who expressed their basic idea in its most detached and philosophical form, they held that conduct was three-fourths of life."[23] There was no question in Chesterton's mind that what we are is extremely important, but he was also quite well aware that it is by what we *do* that we become what we *are*—and this bespeaks ethics (or morality) as the cardinal concern. It was a cardinal concern of the Victorians even when it was no longer supported by religion; it was the cardinal concern of Chesterton that led him back to religion.

It is important to emphasize this concern in Chesterton if we are not to be misled by Marshall McLuhan's characterization (or caricature) of Chesterton in the Introduction to Hugh Kenner's profoundly perceptive book, *Paradox in Chesterton*, as a "metaphysical moralist, who, because presumably he was concerned with contemplating a world he had not made, was not concerned with shaping the minds of human beings and thus, even if only indirectly, shaping a world in which human beings live."[24] It should be stressed in this connection that, for Chesterton, human behavior was significant, precisely as human, only to the extent that it was spiritual, self-determining activity. Any attempts to modify behavior by means of physical changes in the human organism or to breed what might seem to be desirable physical characteristics were anathema to him. Education, yes; eugenics or behaviorism, no. It should also be noted, by the way, that Chesterton was not lamentably lagging behind the times by emphasizing the importance of the content of what is handed on in the educational process. It could seem he was missing the point of deriving the very concept of education from the activity of "drawing-out," as opposed to "putting-in."[25] He had little sympathy with either the Platonic *myth* of "reminiscence" (ἀνάμνησις) or the Hegelian *concept* of the "a priori" (the latter, by the way, not the Kantian concept). In a certain sense, perhaps, he was missing the point, but at the same time he was making an equally important point. Overemphasis on the aspect of drawing-out can lead to a failure in the courage to affirm that there are truths that are simply not already *in* the mind to be educated but are to be brought about by a process wherein one who does not know is led to know by someone who does know. We do not, in fact, know exactly what that process is, but we do know that it does not happen without the intervention of a teacher—a teacher who has knowledge—and we do also know that the teacher does not literally "put" the knowledge in.

MORAL EDUCATION

There is no question here of imputing to Chesterton a theory of education in general. His primary concern is moral education, and that is a question of learning how to make the right choices, which inevitably involves knowing what the right choices to be made are—and that does not mean "doing what comes naturally." Everything he ever wrote contained a message, and the message was always a moral message. One need not say that Chesterton was always right in moral matters, but one does have to say that what he constantly sought to bring about was what he thought was morally right. It is, of course, not easy to say exactly what *knowing* is in the moral order, but we can say (1) that it is *not* "scientific" and that it would be ludicrous to demand scientific knowledge of the morally right; (2) that moral knowing is not mere guessing; we not only know abstractly the difference between right and wrong, but for the most part we can know concretely what we must or must not do; and (3) that, despite enormous individual differences among human beings, generalization in moral matters is absolutely essential, if we are not to give way to the barbarism of arbitrariness. In short, there must be a moral code that binds all alike in things that really matter; "ought" is not a meaningless monosyllable. We have heard so much in recent times of the relativity of moral convictions to historical, social, and cultural conditions that we run the risk of concluding that there are no moral absolutes whatever; that we of the West in the twentieth century and the "First World" have no right to criticize cultures that gloried in human sacrifice, the mutilation of captives, or the degradation of women; that we have no right to judge that these things are wrong in any age, any society, any culture. "The only true free-thinker is he whose intellect is as much free from the future as from the past. He cares as little for what will be as for what has been; he cares only for what ought to be."[26] Nor is moral ought to be confused with aesthetic preference. Chesterton was among those who regarded writing itself as having a moral purpose, to which its aesthetic purpose is subordinate—one of the reasons he was so enamored of medieval art, with its conscious moral purpose.

Those who think—with Maisie Ward, for example—that he should have abandoned journalism and devoted himself to literature, simply do not understand that he could not do that and still be G. K. Chesterton; only as a journalist could he "do his thing." It may very well be that his uncompromising championing of morality could make him unpopular with a certain segment of modern society; popularity was not what he sought, truth was. "If our aunts ought to have been able to hear of immorality without fainting, surely our nephews might brace themselves to hear about morality without throwing an epileptic fit."[27] The whole point he is constantly trying to make is that moral judgments are objectively true or false, and no amount of thinking—no matter whose—is going to change that. The failure to see this is simply a mental misfortune. "As we should be genuinely sorry for tramps and paupers who are materially homeless, so we should be sorry for those who are morally homeless, and who suffer a philosophical starvation as deadly as physical starvation."[28] The point, however, is not that there is an objective moral code "out there," so to speak, to be imposed on all of us by law and force; rather it is that the validity of moral thinking and, thus, of moral behavior is independent of external sanctions. Law does not dictate morality; morality dictates law—despite what American "legal positivists" might think. It should be added here, however, that in Chesterton's view, especially after his conversion to Roman Catholicism, there does exist authoritative moral teaching, which sound rational thinking will find to be correct.[29] One has to wonder, of course, along with Chesterton, just how "sound" "rational thinking" will be without a solid foundation of faith, unless, of course, we think—again along with Chesterton—that the solid religious foundation is itself a demand of "sound rational thinking." As Dale has pointed out perceptively, the Chestertons—both Gilbert and Cecil—thought ethically *before* they thought religiously or theologically.[30] We must, of course, recognize that not only is morality a demand of sound religious thinking—an immoral demand is *eo ipso* an irreligious demand—but religion is a demand of sound moral thinking. It may be that the person who is not religious is not morally at fault, but one does have to wonder whether he or she is morally obtuse.

That the concept of morality had such hard sledding in Chesterton's day—which is not to say that people, even philosophers, were more immoral than in other ages—is to a large extent due to a mental mixup on the question of values. To speak of morality in any meaningful sense, after all, is to speak of moral values, of the oughtness that attaches to them. If, however, we begin by focusing on the verb rather than on the noun "value," we immediately run the risk of subjectifying the noun, and that in a very muddled sort of way. Valuing (or evaluating) is unquestionably the activity of a subject, of a spiritual subject, just as thinking is. Now, there is nothing particularly modern in the dilemma as to what causes what, when there is question of subjective activity. Historically speaking, it would seem, the confusion regarding the relation of subject and object dates back to the Sophists, who got a great deal of mileage out of subjectifying the object valued, and, thus, the value objectified in it. One would think that Plato put that confusion to rest early when he has Socrates ask Euthyphro just what the "holiness" is to which the latter appeals to justify his actions. When Euthyphro replies that "the holy is what is pleasing to the gods,"[31] Socrates asks him, "Is it holy because it is pleasing to the gods, or is it pleasing to the gods because it is holy?"[32] But, not only did Socrates not put the sophism to rest for all time; it has remained a favorite of sceptics in all ages. Perhaps it is natural that it should, which only goes to show that what is natural is not necessarily what is reliable. Chesterton uses a more homely example to get across pretty much the same point as did Plato: When trees wave in the wind, we perceive the movement of the wind and the movement of the trees. We might just be tempted to think, he says, as apparently the materialists do, that the trees are moving the wind, but any "sane" person knows that the wind is moving the trees. The confusion is the result of a mixed-up concept of "cause." Chesterton does not speak of confusing an epistemological and an ontological concept of cause (or of saying "*be*cause"), but that is what he is talking about. If someone asks you, "How do you know it is cold outside?" You might well reply, "Because there are icicles on the window-frame." You both know the difference between judging-because and being-because, and so no harm is done. But, it is not so easy when the question is one of *value*—moral or otherwise. Much has been said these days—and will undoubtedly continue to be said—about the distinction between fact and value, between is and ought, and among a large number of our contemporaries the prize money goes to "fact" and "is," because "value" and "ought," being subjective, cannot be verified. Science, we are told, is and should be "value-free," which may very well be quite true, but that is just another reason to make sure that we do not look to science to guide life. We might, in fact, counter with, "Values are and should be science-free." It may also be very true that moral conclusions differ from age to age, from culture to culture, from social group to social group, or even from individual to individual; this does not mean that moral standards are arbitrary. As Chesterton says, "Teetotallers say that wine is bad because they think it moral to say what they think. Christians will not say that wine is bad because they think it immoral to say what they don't think.[33]

SUBJECTIVITY AND MORALITY

Here it is that a different form of subjectivity may be invoked as a guarantee of the objectivity of moral judgment. No one recognized more keenly than Aristotle the difficulty of making accurate particular moral judgments. The general rule is that we should always try to do what is good, at the same time recognizing that it is not easy to be sure that what appears to us to be good really is good. For this reason he invoked two moral rules which could well not seem rational at all. The first of these is that we can judge what is good by seeing what the good person does, seeing in such a person the very criterion of goodness.[34] There are, it would seem, persons whom we cannot but recognize as good, as "virtuous"—Socrates would be an example—whose way of acting becomes a kind of proof of the goodness of the acting. It could well seem that the principle he is appealing to is more religious than rational, but that says nothing against its validity. The second rule tells us that we are guided in our choices by our character, which character *can* make what is not good appear to us to be good, thus seemingly making the choice of the good "involuntary." But this does so *only* seemingly, because it is by our choices that we form the character that is ours, and "involuntary" choice makes no sense whatever.[35] This, by the way, contains an affirmation, both that there *is* a real good and that it is *objective*, without claiming that it is easy to know. Chesterton, too, sees character as a force that can guide the accuracy of moral judgment: e.g., the judgment of the consistently honest person, not the judgment of one for whom honesty is a "policy" (even "the best policy")—it simply cannot be a "policy" at all. There is also significance in the fact that truly virtuous people experience a *feeling* of repugnance when faced with an opportunity to do what is objectively immoral, which simply means that we should take seriously both the subjectivity of objectivity and the objectivity of subjectivity.

Although I am not aware that Chesterton ever adverts to the etymology of the term ethics, derived as it is from the Greek term ἦθος, which means "character," not from ἔθος, which means "custom," it is quite clear that his approach to morality is guided by the Aristotelian insight into τὰ ἠθικά, the matters that pertain to character. This is one reason why Chesterton in everything he wrote, be it poetry, fiction, literary criticism, biography, apologetics, social criticism, political commentary, economics, or just plain philosophy, was keenly aware of his moral responsibility to his audience—for him, "art for art's sake" is simply a moral absurdity, perhaps even an aesthetic absurdity. This might, in the eyes of some, detract from the literary value of what he wrote, but he was simply far more concerned with ethics than with aesthetics. Thus, his attitude toward the evil he finds abounding in the society of his day is not one of elegant literary portrayal but of righteous indignation. Chesterton was an artist—that no one can take from him—but it would never occur to him that art could be "for art's sake," no more than it could be for the artist's sake; it could only be for the sake of the beholders—however that term is to be interpreted. One sees this so well particularly in Chesterton's work of literary criticism, where he is far more concerned with what the literary figure, be he Browning or Blake or Chaucer, does *for* his readers than in how he expresses himself; art is not merely self-expression, it is communication. There may conceivably be a sense in which science is value-free; it is clearly difficult to think of art as being value-free, not merely in the sense that beauty is indisputably a value, but also in the sense that the moral dimensions of art are inescapable. Chesterton was not happy with the attempts of some of his contemporaries to equate morality with taste, but he would not and could not deny that the moral dimensions of taste are significant; moral evil involves moral bad taste. This is one of the reasons why Chesterton resonates so well with Charles Dickens and Robert Browning, to say nothing of Francis of Assisi and Thomas Aquinas. He sees good morality as a demand of the moral nature of the human, and he is convinced, along with Plato, Aristotle, and Thomas Aquinas, that the human mind can probe objectively the moral nature of the human. It is for this reason that everything Chesterton wrote was guided by moral purpose. It is for this reason, too, that he was convinced that one could appreciate Shakespeare's art only if one could know and appreciate Shakespeare's morality. Thus, to attempt a Freudian interpretation of Shakespeare's characters is simply sheer nonsense;[36] it is to impute to Shakespeare both a morality and a psychology he never heard of. It not only makes no sense to psychoanalyze Hamlet; it makes even less sense to psychoanalyze Shakespeare. But it makes a great deal of sense to try to understand Hamlet in the light of Shakespeare's moral concept of duty, or Lear in the light of Shakespeare's moral judgment of ingratitude.

This, it would seem, leads imperceptably back to a consideration of the so-called opposition between the theoretical and the practical, the former characterized by thinking, the latter by action. Given a serious problem, we are told, the theoretical type thinks about it, while the practical type does something about it. Chesterton, however, would say that it is highly impractical to do anything about anything without first thinking about it, without thinking out the implications of any proposed action. It is precisely when a problem is really serious that the question is not that of doing *something* about it; the question is that of doing the *right* thing about it, and that can require profound theoretical thought.[37] The practical person is not the one who emphasizes *doing*, rather it is the one who emphasizes *what* is done (or to be done), and the "what" can demand a great deal of thinking out. The "thinking out," in turn, demands a concrete grasp of the actual situation calling for action, all the way from choosing the right coat to wear when the temperature is 45° and it is raining, to choosing the economic policy that is most likely to provide a solution to the problem of poverty in New York City, or Paris, or London, for the foreseeable future.

It may very well be that in the long run deeds are preferable to words, but it just might also be that words will stimulate the thoughts without which the deeds may turn out to be more harmful than helpful.[38] There are good and less good ways of formulating moral demands. Chesterton has many a striking thing to say in ringing the changes on that vaguest of notions, the notion of "progress," so dear to his own generation—today we are somewhat less sanguine about it. One of the most fundamental principles of Chesterton's thinking is the unshakable conviction that "progress" is meaningful only as the improvement of human living, a corollary to which is that technological advances do not necessarily bring with them improvement in human living—no more than they necessarily involve degradation of the same. The problem, of course, is the basic problem of morality: what constitutes an improvement in human living? The answer: *quot homines, tot sententiae.* Some will say pleasure, others will say success, still others wealth, or power, or reputation, and some might even contend that it is virtue, which is our way of translating the Platonic–Aristotelian notion of ἀρετή, which is "excellence" at being human. To add to the complexity of the matter, what people *say* may have little to do with how people *act,* and the *acting* may be either worse or better than the *saying.* Some may *say* that virtue is what counts, and what they pursue may be constant self-aggrandizement. Others may *say* that pleasure is what counts, and the pleasure they seek may be the pleasure of making others happy. What makes all of this so difficult is that words are going to solve nothing, nor, for the most part, is argument. The way we see things can to a very great extent be unaffected by the way we—or anyone else—say things. And here is where Chesterton comes in. So much of what he *says* may justifiably be, from the logical point of view, gratuitous assertion, but the *way* he says it may enable us to *see* what he cannot *prove.*

We all know deep down in our hearts that change is not necessarily improvement, but we live in an advertising culture that constantly presents change as *eo ipso* improvement. Chesterton says, they "talk as if the change were unchangeable,"[39] and, as it were, a light goes on in our head. When he continues, "the very latest opinion is always infallibly right and always inevitably wrong,"[40] we know that, even though as a generalization this does not hold water, it does make us *see* differently, and, it can be hoped, seeing differently will mean acting differently. It is as though Chesterton is saying for us what we should like to have said ourselves. Who of us who are old enough to remember have not had the experience? "It is right because a new generation of young people are tired of things and wrong because another generation of young people

lamities."[44] One could well ask, who in our contemporary society makes our moral judgments for us?

STABILITY AND CHANGE

If, then, change is to be evaluated, as it would seem it must, the evaluation will make sense only if what changes also remains the same, and only if there is at least a relatively permanent standard of evaluation which we call an "ideal." Without ideals there is no criterion for judging whether change is progress or retrogression, and without agreement on ideals there is no possibility of discussion.[45] In this connection it will be not without significance to emphasize the close relationship of *idea* and *ideal*, particularly as Chesterton employs the two terms. Both terms have the seemingly contradictory connotations of *image* and *exemplar*, such that each is at once a "copy" of the reality it represents and a "model" which the reality in question instantiates, the "eternal image"[46] that is "prior" to the particulars that realize it. Chesterton illustrates this very pointedly by referring to what might seem to be a contradiction in the biblical account of creation, according to which light was created *before* the sun and the stars. "One could not imagine a process more open to the elephantine logic of the Bible-smasher than this: that the sun should be created after the sunlight."[47] There simply has to be a sense in which the idea of light is prior to the concrete light that is the sun. What is at issue, however, is not the relation of exemplar to things but rather the relation of a standard of value to the realization that is to be judged. If, for example, it is agreed that light is a value, then its existence may very well depend on the existence of the sun; its value does not. "But the point is that when the critic calls the present good or bad, he ought to be comparing it with the ideal and not with the rather dismal reality called himself."[48] Presumably, no matter what our theories may be, we all make value-judgments, chief of which are judgments of moral value, even though our concept of "moral value" may be very much mixed up. It may be, too, that we prefer to think of values as subjective, a matter of convention, or even of fad or fancy, but we ought to be able to see that that way leads to chaos, anarchy. If we really care for what is right we cannot be content to compare one convention with another; each convention must be scrutinized in the light of right reason.[49] If change is to be evaluated at all, the standard of evaluation must in some intelligible sense be permanent.[50] There is, to be sure, a sense in which Chesterton can and should be called an "idealist," in the sense of one who put a constant emphasis on the primacy of the idea (ideal, exemplar, paradigm), but always with feet firmly planted in the homely—and homey—solidity of material reality. It is also true that he can legitimately be called a "realist" in his conviction that the complementarity of spirit and matter is such that failure to recognize the primacy of spirit is to tread the narrow—and narrowing—path that leads to insanity.

One result of Chesterton's constant insistence on the permanence of ideals is that he has frequently been charged (a) with idealizing the Middle Ages and (b) with wanting to restore that period in history. Both of these allegations are understandable but superficial. He did *not* idealize the Middle Ages. What he did was to find in the Middle Ages an idea of society, imperfectly realized then, but not realized at all in the modern age. One might convince oneself that, in novels like *The Napoleon of Notting Hill* and *The Ball and the Cross*, Chesterton was pining for the return of medievalism, but he was not; he quite clearly rejects the romantic notion that such a social order should or could be restored. What he does think, however, is that the medieval ideal is still valid and worthy of a better realization. Integrity, to take but one example, does not cease to be an ideal, no matter how imperfect its realization. It might be added that Chesterton was very much aware that any "ism" is bound to be one-sided and therefore in need of reform—or reformulation. Even if we grant that Chesterton himself sometimes made the wrong practical choices in relation to his ideals, that in itself does not invalidate the ideals.

To speak of ideals and their significance as goals to be reached for is to put one's finger on an ever-recurring theme in Chesterton's productive life, the indignant re-jection of pessimism in any and all of its forms. This is not to say that he was unaware that there is evil—a great deal of it—in this world. His life was one continuous campaign against the evils he perceived, one of the chief of which was the denial that there is good in the world, the denial that life is basically good. It may be purely coincidental, but it is unquestionably illuminating that on June 13, 1936 (the day before he died) there appeared in *The Illustrated London News* an article of his con-taining the following sentence: "It [*The Man Who Was Thursday*] was intended to describe the world of wild doubt and despair which the pessimists were generally describing at that date; with just a gleam of hope in some double meaning of the doubt, which even the pessimists felt in some fitful fashion." *The Man Who Was Thurs-day* appeared in 1908, the same year as *Orthodoxy*, and the above remark speaks of a whole career devoted to combating pessimism. In *Avowals and Denials*, 1934, he has this to say: "There was any amount of pessimism in the period in which I began to write. In fact, it was largely because of the pessimism that I did begin to write."[51] Then comes the twist that makes this vintage Chesterton: "The mere fact that I did begin to write, naturally, will be used as another argument on the side of the pessimists."[52] We may or may not be convinced that there is any need to repeat this today, since we may not see pessimism as today's problem, but since cynicism is today's problem, and cynicism is very close to pessimism, the aptness of what Chesterton says remains. The heart of pessimism is not the acknowledgment that ideals are but imperfectly realized, but the fact that ideals are simply denied; that, because human life is simply not worthwhile, ideals have no meaning whatever. It is for this reason, says Chesterton, that pessimists are to be sharply distinguished from reformers; no one seeks to improve what one does not love; and this is to assert "the eternal and essential truth that until we love a thing in all its ugliness we cannot make it beautiful"[53]—first the loving, then the effort to improve, and the pessimist does not love. "The cause which is blocking all progress today is the subtle scepticism which whispers in a million ears that things are not good enough to be worth improving";[54] that in 1901. We begin to see, then, that optimism is not a rational conviction but a character trait, the intellectual working-out of which is not its source but its "symptoms."[55] He later says of Dickens (1906) what he here says of Browning (1903), both of whom get to us because they share the same enthusiasm for life.[56] The pessimist, it would seem, has no enthusiasm for anything, least of all for life. According to Maisie Ward, Chesterton characterized pessimism as a "paralysis of the mind, an impotence intrinsically unworthy of a free man."[57] The patent existence of evil—of a great deal of it—provides no argument for the nonexistence of good, nor does the realistic recognition that the world will never be completely rid of evil.[58] We can and must be sorry that there is much evil in the world, but we must also realize that "Sorrow and pessimism are by their natures opposites: sorrow rests on the value of something; pessimism on the value of nothing."[59]

It is easy enough to say, of course, that there is no way of proving that the world is good, that the experience of the universe should make us joyful. By the same token there is no way of proving the opposite, so that the question of "proving" anything in this matter ends in a stalemate. It is not easy to understand why anyone would prefer to affirm a predominance of disvalues in the world, but it is even more difficult to understand why anyone would think that the presence of evil in the world proves the absence of good; one could go so far as to say that it is meaningless to speak of evil if there is no good to which it is contrasted. This, incidentally, indicates why the pessimist can never be a reformer; the pessimist does not know if it is worthwhile—or perhaps "knows" that it is not worthwhile. "While the eye that can perceive what are the wrong things increases in an uncanny and devouring clarity, the eye which sees what things are right is growing mistier and mistier every moment, till it goes almost blind with doubt."[60] What is important to note, Chesterton assures us, is that pain, suffering, and sorrow are not the experiences that produce pessimism; many a pessimist is materially well off—only spiritually impoverished. "Sorrow and pessimism are indeed, in a sense, opposite things, since sorrow is founded on the value of something, and pessimism on the value of nothing."[61] Dickens was not optimistic because he was successful; he was successful because he was optimistic. Pessimism, on the other hand, is empty; nothing follows from it.[62]

THE REFUSAL OF NEGATION

Here it is that the real Chesterton emerges in all his immensity. His appreciation of life, his joy in existence could not be taken from him. It was not that he ignored pain and sorrow and evil; it was simply that he would not let them take joy from him. It may be, of course, that people who are just plain happy all the time can become quite banal, even annoying, but that was not the case with Chesterton: he simply radiated a joy that was so authentic that it made others joyful. One of his very best friends, E. C. Bentley, said of him that he was "by nature the happiest boy and man I have ever known; even in the adolescent phase of morbid misery that so many of us go through . . . laughter was never far away."[63] Chesterton's own contention was that joy is more natural to the human condition than sadness is; he found more joy among the poor who were light-hearted than among the rich who were heavy-handed. Out of joy springs praise—provided joy is seen as a gift: "Man is more himself, man is more manlike, when joy is the fundamental thing in him, and grief the superficial. Melancholy should be an innocent interlude, a tender and fugitive frame of mind; praise should be the permanent pulsation of the soul."[64] One might be inclined to read into these words either exaggeration or insensitivity, but actually it comes from one who was "sympathetic" in the original sense of the term; he "felt with" the experiences of others, he experienced both their sorrow and their joy, but he rejoiced to be able to do so; he radiated joy—in all seriousness. It may be that we are all moved profoundly by Hamlet's words, "To be or not to be. That is the question," but, says Chesterton, St. Thomas Aquinas' words are even more moving when the massive medieval doctor thunders, "To be, that is the answer."[65]

To be alive is simply an astounding gift, and Chesterton never ceased to acclaim the glory of existence, never ceased saying yes to life, never ceased being thankful for it, with all its imperfections. It was for this very reason that he found the basic attitude of the Middle Ages—particularly the English Middle Ages—so enticing. In this he has been criticized—chiefly by those who see the Middle Ages as the "Dark Ages"—for a blindness to medieval faults and an idealization of medieval virtues, which together constitute unrealistic desire to return to the Middle Ages. It is quite possible, of course, that Chesterton overestimated the Middle Ages—although in praising this period in history his emphasis was chiefly on its art (architecture and poetry), its philosophy, and its theology, in which he was quite correct—but he was by no means pining for a return to its political, social, and educational system; he quite clearly recognized that there was much in the Middle Ages that was undeveloped. "Men with medieval sympathies are sometimes accused, absurdly enough, of trying to prove that the medieval period was perfect. In truth the whole case for it is that it was imperfect";[66] in it the fruit was not yet ripe.[67] Far more important than any glorification of the Middle Ages was his constant reminder, particularly to the English, that the Gothic architecture that dots the English countryside bears testimony not only to the artistic genius of its creators, not only to its high culture (which included the mathematical),[68] but also to the role of monasticism in the civilizing of the Britons.[69]

It is difficult to say whether it was Chesterton's growing attachment to the Roman Catholic Church that made him sympathetic to the medieval spirit, or his ability to resonate with Chaucer, Francis of Assisi, Thomas Aquinas, and Dante that drew him gradually more and more to Catholicism. It is not without significance, to be sure, that his masterful books on Chaucer and Thomas Aquinas were written considerably after his conversion to Catholicism, and even Francis of Assisi came shortly after that conversion, but those facts do not answer the question; still, in any event there is some sort of connection.

One thing is clear: he saw conversion as a call *to* rationality rather than away *from* it, a rationality which he found far more manifest in the Middle Ages than in the rationalistic "Enlightenment" of the eighteenth century or of the Victorian era. He made a very clear distinction between rationality and rationalism; of the latter he is severely critical. In his book on Chaucer he writes: "In this book I advance the general thesis, that, in spite of everything, there was a balanced philosophy in medieval times; and some very unbalanced philosophies in later times."[70] To put it quite simply, he found more straightforward philosophizing and less confusing rhetoric among the medievals than he did among the "rationalists": "Even here we feel something of that *communis sententia,* or medieval common sense, which was so much less rhetorical and therefore so much more really rational than the rational eighteenth century."[71] By the same token, he finds that medieval art, particularly its poetry and its architecture (medieval music was practically unknown to Chesterton's generation), recognizes its "responsibility to society,"[72] which, of course, makes sense only if the role of art is to *communicate* objectivity, not merely to *express* subjectivity: "But the moment of creation (artistic) is the moment of communication. It is when the work has passed from mind to mind that it becomes a work of art."[73] More than that, he is convinced that the high art, as well as the philosophy and theology, of the Middle Ages springs from the profound spiritual center that is religion: "In short it is my general aim throughout to show that all these artistic manifestations spring from deep spiritual energies in the religious centre itself; and this is why they seem at first sight to be insolently proud of that centre as a centre of civilization."[74] It is not difficult to see, then, that Chesterton's return to the Middle

Ages is not a retreat from reason but a recapturing of spiritual balance, from which the superstitions of science have been an unbalanced retreat. It would also be misguided to look upon Chesterton as simply anti-modern in his attitudes toward art, science, and philosophy; quite simply, he could not abide uncritical modernity.

4

The Superstitions of Science

WHEN WE LOOK TODAY at the Victorian Age with its three divinities, science, progress, and prosperity, we may be inclined to wonder how anyone ever took that triad seriously, especially since we now know that science has seen greater advances in the past thirty years than it did in the history that stretches from Archimedes to Einstein; that progress is for the most part illusory, not a process of humanization; and that prosperity is almost exclusively "the prosperity of the prosperous."[1] In the first three decades of this century, however, when G. K. Chesterton *floruit*, it was not so, at least among "intellectuals" who cared little or nothing for either the experiences or the opinions of the "common man." It is important, then, to note that from the time he first emerged into prominence, between 1900 and 1901, to his death in 1936 Chesterton was ceaselessly in the forefront of opposition to these superstitutions, these optimisms—not, however, as we have already seen, from the point of view of the crusading pessimist, but with the blazing zeal of the reformer who would challenge the human spirit to recapture its birthright. That birthright, he became more and more convinced, was essentially supernatural, but it was constantly under fire from the unspiritual spirit of the age to which he belonged. What seems to have happened is that the spirit of "wonder," of which Aristotle speaks and which causes human beings to ask questions with a reasonable hope of coming up with reasonable but not necessarily "certain" answers, had turned into the conviction that "science," as understood in the eighteenth-century "Enlightenment" and as developed in the technological revolution of the nineteenth and twentieth centuries, has precluded the necessity of ongoing wonder, because ultimately science will find all the answers that are to be found. If science cannot find answers, there are no answers to be found, and to ask questions that science cannot answer is to engage in superstition.

It is as though in the nineteenth and twentieth centuries there was emerging out of the seeming contradiction of the rationalism and utilitarianism of the eighteenth century a phenomenal confidence in the human mind's capacity not to solve mysteries but to do away with them— a way, after all, of solving them. Thus there arose, alongside the legitimate sciences of the mathematically measurable, not only the quasi-scientific social sciences, where measurement was a potent help but not an infallible guide, since "measuring" human behavior cannot be authentically scientific, but pseudo-sciences like phrenology, physiognomy, palmistry, graphology, heredity, and eugenics, to mention but the most prominent, which were actually contra-scientific. It is important to repeat, incidentally, that Chesterton was neither anti-scientific nor unscientific—even though his knowledge of science was for the most part rudimentary. He had two main concerns in this regard: (1) that science not be expected to do what it was not geared to do, and (2) that the pseudo-sciences be recognized for what they are and not be raised to the dignity of authentic science, where they did great harm. Science, he was convinced, could provide us with many legitimate answers to legitimate questions, but science could not tell us what to do with the answers; only wisdom could do that, a wisdom not coterminous with science.

Before going any further it is important to put to rest

the suspicion entertained by a great many anti-Chestertonians that Chesterton was reactionary in his attitude toward evolution, denying that it was scientific or that there was adequate evidence to support the theory. Chesterton did not, in fact, attack the theory of evolution at all; he saw no need either to attack or to defend it. What he did was to attack light-headed evolutionists who thought that the theory explained far more than it could, a fault, incidentally, which Chesterton did not impute to Charles Darwin himself. What concerned Chesterton was not the truth or falsity of the theory but rather its importance as explanatory, and explanatory of what. Evolution is not a force that brings about change; it is a process, which can be up to a point described, the process wherein change comes about. It has not one legitimate word to say about the source of the process. Evolution produces nothing; at best it is a mode of production. "To state the process is scarcely to state the agent."[2] "If evolution simply means that a positive thing called an ape turned very slowly into a positive thing called a man, then it is stingless for the most orthodox; for a personal God might just as well do things slowly, as quickly, especially if, like the Christian God, he were outside time."[3] Unlike many of his followers, Darwin himself, Chesterton tells us, was very much aware that the "Missing Link" stood for a gap in the theory, not invalidating it, but not allowing us to be too sanguine about the explanatory force of the theory, precisely because what is "missing" explains nothing. The Darwinian dogmatists "talk of searching for the habits or habitat of the Missing Link; as if one were to talk of being on friendly terms with the gap in a narrative and the hole in an argument, of taking a walk with a *nonsequitur* or dining with an undistributed middle."[4] Heavy-handed satire, admittedly, but those of us who are old enough to have seen the descriptions—and even drawings—of stages in the evolutionary process produced in the early decades of this century can appreciate the need of just such satire. Someone, after all, had to make fun of such things as H. G. Wells' *Outline of History*, where the whole of history is turned into a process of things getting constantly better and better—culminating in Edwardian England!

What Chesterton has put his finger on so adroitly is the fallacy whereby unscientific epigones turn a theory into something more important than what it is presumed to explain, transforming the *de*scriptive force of a plausible hypothesis into the *pre*scriptive force of a necessary "law," or a system of necessary laws. It is this sort of nonsense which even today permits self-styled "scientists" who write reviews for the Sunday *Times* to claim that any appeal to transcendence is not worthy of discussion among genuine "intellectuals." To speak of the physical evolution of an organism is one thing; to speak of the evolution of the idea of God in the brain of an evolving organism, as does Wells, is simply to go beyond the evidence available for the sake of a theory which must be presumed to be universal in its application—development and evolution are simply not synonymous.[5] Chesterton's opposition to this sort of thing, however, is even more sweeping in its rejection of the claim by some "scientists" to know far more about primitive man than they do, their supposition being that to say "primitive" is to say "barbaric" or "undeveloped." It is simply *a priori* arbitrariness, says Chesterton, to assume that "every obvious human custom is a relic of some base and barbaric custom."[6] In addition to this, there is the illegitimate interpretation of the evidence that is available, as though the interpreter knows what the primitive mind intended. In *The Everlasting Man* Chesterton devotes considerable space, as we have seen, to the relatively sophisticated artistry in the drawings in the prehistoric caves of southern France. Presumably prehistoric men (the "savages") intended to make drawings, not diagrams, and in so doing they manifested both remarkable powers of observation and remarkable drawing skill, even artistic creativity. The point is that "the student cannot make a scientific statement about the savage, because the 'savage' is not making a scientific statement about the world."[7] We might add that he is most probably enjoying himself immensely in doing what he is doing, learning a great deal about himself while he is at it, and giving a great deal of aesthetic pleasure to other "savages"—even though he is not making scientific statements even about himself.

To make a thoroughly illegitimate use of a perfectly legitimate theory such as evolution, however, is a far cry from cooking up a pseudo-science and then to claim as "scientific" the conclusions drawn from non-evidence. There is no need to dispute the validity—or at least plausibility—of behavioral studies on both the individual and the social levels. Patterns of behavior can be studied, and conclusions can be drawn from them. But, it is simply unscientific—and frequently immoral—to examine antecedent physical configurations and to predict from them subsequent behavior patterns. Once again, of course, things are not so bad now as they were in Chesterton's day, but it may well have been that he had a good deal to do with laying these ghosts to rest. It may be that the pseudo-sciences of physiognomy and phrenology did not long survive the devastating criticism of them by Hegel— although Hegel's concept of the human *spirit* has had rough sledding even in more recent times—but the pseudo-sciences have survived in more modified form in some of the worst aspects of criminology, heredity, and eugenics—to say nothing of the more recent genetic engineering.

What needs to be emphasized is the clearcut distinction between matter and spirit—without falling into an indefensible sort of dualism that exaggeratedly separates the two. If the reality of the spiritual can be reduced to a refined and complex functioning of the material, then a scientific study of the human organism should be able to tell us all we need to know about the human person. Since, however, it is obviously not true that the face, the cranium, or the genetic heritage of an individual will reveal to us all that we need to know about even the probable behavior of that individual, we should be very reluctant to label "scientific" a study of such physical factors. We should be even more reluctant to pass judgment on the probable moral character of the individual based on the desirability or undesirability of certain physical characteristics. It is true enough, as Chesterton would admit, that we can successfully breed racehorses, or prize dogs or pigs, nor need we judge the moral character of the breeder, but we cannot breed human goodness—not even human intelligence—and even if we could, it would be immoral to do so: witness the Nazi experiments. Now, it takes no great intelligence either to understand or to express this sort of argument, but it takes great wit—such as Chesterton's—to get the point across strikingly and to make people *see* what mere argument will not make them see. Frequently he is at his most humorous and, it must be admitted, his most heavy-handed in dealing with such aberrations.

SCIENCE AND IDEOLOGY

It may, of course, seem to us today that, important as was Chesterton's witness in the first three decades of this century, he has little to say to us, since the problems he was dealing with are not our problems. The point, however, is not that we are today dealing with the same specific issues that Chesterton was, but that the overall issue of the relation of science and technology to human freedom continues to be a live issue to which Chesterton still speaks. Science is still a sacred cow, and ever-advancing technology more and more calls the shots in human living. There is a very real sense in which Chesterton was in his day a prophet, not so much by way of foresight and prediction but by clearly seeing the perils of rampant secularism and by lashing out against it in ways that still make sense. No one, for example, saw more clearly than Chesterton the evils of capitalism, which in his day was only a shadow of what it is today in its control of human behavior and human destinies through concentrated ownership. By the same token, however, he was almost unique in his awareness that socialist collectivism was but the obverse side of the capitalist coin, offering no more authentic freedom than does capitalism, but merely another form of the all-powerful state, and also controlling human behavior and restraining freedom. It may be that his dream of "Distributism," to which we shall return later, was not a very realistic answer to the twofold problem, but it contained a more humane ideal of human living than either of the other two. In what might be called a more concrete way, Chesterton saw the Armistice of 1918 for exactly what it was, a mere interlude in Germany's threat to the world, a significant insight, even though predicated on a rather arrogant contention that Germany was uniquely responsible for World War I. In essay after essay, collected in a book entitled *The End of the Armistice*, he analyzed that threat, not so much by way of predicting what was to happen in the future as by seeing what was already in the process of coming about. Thus, although he did not live to see the actual beginning of World War II, he wrote of it as beginning with an attack on Poland by Germany—in agreement with Russia![8] "He had formed a certain theory of Germany—part of a larger theory of Europe—and everything that happened from 1914 to his death in 1936 confirmed it, though not so spectacularly as it has been confirmed by all that has happened since."[9] Chesterton's own words written about the prophetic spirit he saw in William Cobbett contain a striking parallel to his own prophetic spirit.

> What he [Cobbett] saw was the perishing of the whole English power of self-support, the growth of cities that drain and dry up the countryside, the growth of dense dependent populations incapable of finding their own food, the toppling triumph of machines over men, the sprawling omnipotence of financiers over patriots, the herding of humanity in nomadic masses whose very homes are homeless, the terrible necessity of peace and the terrible probability of war, all the loading up of our little island like a sinking ship; the wealth that may mean famine and the culture that may mean despair; the bread of Midas and the sword of Damocles. In a word, he saw what we see, but he saw it when it was not there. And some cannot see it—even when it is there.[10]

It was the same prophetic spirit in him that saw the inevitable cruelty (criminality) of totalitarianism: "Where the State was the sole consideration, it was found in experience that they [people] were much more cruel."[11] It is possible to speak legitimately of the needs of society, but it is not legitimate that the needs of society should eliminate the rights of individuals.

If we are to understand much of what Chesterton has to say about individual and society, morality, religion, and politics, art and science, we shall have to come to grips with his thought concerning the reality of spirit and the spiritual. Here, however, we are at a disadvantage: if we want to follow his thought on any topic, we shall find that he is quite capable of thinking very systematically; he sees truth as a gigantic network of interrelated truths, each implying all and all implying each. If, however, we want to trace the interrelatedness without falsifying it, we may find the thought more elusive than we initially supposed. I have a theory about the reasons for this which I present quite tentatively, because I have not found either Chesterton or his commentators saying exactly this. As I see it, Chesterton thinks quite philosophically, in the sense that his thinking, at least from 1900 on, is constantly informed by a logic which is traceable, but which might better be called a logic of seeing rather than a logic of inference. On the other hand, Chesterton does not, strictly speaking, think *about* thinking philosophically: he has no theory of philosophical method, with the result that he tells us quite lucidly *what* he thinks without telling us much at all of *how* he thinks, or of how he came to think that way. It is not that we cannot detect an operative method in his thinking and writing—call it, perhaps, "dialectic"—but that he never calls it or describes it as a *method*. As he sees it, then, there is every reason in the world to believe in the existence of spiritual beings; to speak of "reasons" and "believe" is to speak of activities that make sense only as spiritual. On the other hand, there is no reason at all to claim that the only spiritual beings there are are also corporeal; he quite clearly believes in spirits—both good and bad—that are not human spirits. It might be claiming too much to say that for Chesterton there is no dualistic dichotomy of spirit and matter—he does, after all, distinguish between soul and body—but his thinking does not require that distinction bespeak separation, to say nothing of opposition or antagonism. The point that needs to be stressed over and over again— and this Chesterton does—is that to look upon the human as material and material only, as a being of nature and only a being of nature, is to truncate the truly human. The whole of *The Everlasting Man*, one of Chesterton's most philosophical works, was conceived and executed as a thrilling testimony to the spirituality of the human. Because in the English language there are two terms, "mind" and "spirit," which are not necessarily synonymous, there has been a tendency in Anglo-Saxon philosophy, traceable back to Locke and Hume, to speak of mind as though it need not be a spiritual reality, or to speak of a "philosophy of mind" as though such a philosophy could simply ignore the reality of spirit. It was Chesterton's contention, on the other hand, that such an attitude could never come to grips with the reality of the human: "Now the modern Anthropologists, who called themselves Agnostics, completely failed to be Anthropologists at all. Under their limitations, they could not get a complete theory of Man, let alone a complete theory of nature."[12] By the same token he insisted that the materialist mentality—not only in the sense of scientific determinism but also in the sense of an exclusive focus on commodity values—simply cannot understand the human mind at all.[13]

With regard to spiritual reality there are, to be sure, two extremes to be avoided: (1) there are the "spiritualists," of the Arthur Conan Doyle variety, who have set up suspect lines of communication between a spirit world of the deceased and us living mortals; and (2) there are those who have turned "spirit" and "spiritual" into vague metaphors, practically devoid of meaning. As happens so often with Chesterton, he hits the nail on the head in *The Secret of Father Brown*, where he has the little priest–detective reply to the typical agnostic:

> "No, no, no," he said, almost angrily; "I don't mean just a figure of speech. This is what comes of trying to talk about deep things. . . . What's the good of words . . . ? If you try to talk about a truth that's merely moral, people always think it's merely metaphorical. A real live man with two

legs once said to me: 'I only believe in the Holy Ghost in a spiritual sense.' Naturally, I said: 'In what other sense could you believe it?' And *then* he thought I meant he needn't believe in anything except evolution, or ethical fellowship, or some bilge. . . ."[14]

Another danger, of course, is to dismiss all talk of spirit (or spirits)—whether embodied or disembodied—as mere superstition. There simply is no reason to be credulous with regard to the dogma of denial. This is not to say, obviously, that there cannot be superstition in this regard. "The superstition (that is, the unreasoning repugnance and terror) is in the person who admits there can be angels but denies there can be devils. The superstition is in the person who admits there can be devils but denies there can be diabolists."[15] To which might be added—certainly in the Chestertonian spirit—that the authentic believer retains the freedom to affirm or deny, to doubt or reserve judgment on, the presence of either the angelic or the diabolic in concrete situations.

More important for our purposes here than the question of finite spirits other than the human is the question of the adequacy or inadequacy of a study of the human, an anthropology, which leaves out of consideration the human spirit. We all know, of course, that there are those who claim to be anthropologists, or psychologists, or sociologists, moral philosophers, aestheticians, or political philosophers, and who either ignore or deny the reality of the human spirit. It is Chesterton's conviction that they are simply refusing to come to terms with authentic human reality if they do so. Whether or not we want to agree with Chesterton, we shall be unable to come to grips with him at all if we do not realize that he is making the astounding claim, not only that reason demands that we take the human spirit seriously, but that we do so religiously—religion he sees as a *rational* demand, in the

94

sense that reason can see the incompleteness of the human without religion. Speaking of the so-called anthropologists he has this to say:

> But it rapidly became apparent that all sorts of things were Unknowable which were exactly the things that a man has got to know. It is necessary to know whether he is responsible or irresponsible, perfect or imperfect, perfectible or unperfectible, mortal or immortal, doomed or free, not in order to understand God, but in order to understand Man. Nothing that leaves these things under a cloud of religious doubt can possibly pretend to be a Science of Man; it shrinks from anthropology as completely as from theology. Has a man free will; or is his sense of choice an illusion? Has he a conscience, or has his conscience any authority; or is it only the prejudice of the tribal past? Is there any real hope of settling these things by human reason; and has *that* any authority? Is he to regard death as final; and is he to regard miraculous help as possible?[16]

What Chesterton is speaking about here is what issues from the human spirit, each and every human spirit. But there are also spiritual products that issue not so much from the spirit of the individual as from the communal spirit. A revolution can be a spiritual product.[17] A nation is a spiritual product.[18] Resistance to aggression is a spiritual product.[19] The point is: Take away spirit, and what is left of the truly human? We can also look at this from the opposite direction. When Chesterton speaks in *The Everlasting Man*[20] of primitive man drawing pictures of reindeers and of reindeers not drawing pictures of men—or of reindeers—he is, to be sure, saying something about the spirit of man and the non-spirit of the reindeer, but he is also perhaps saying something even more striking; if all he was saying were this, there might well have been no need to say anything. The profound thing is not so much that what he says is true, but that it would not occur to anyone, not to the sceptic, not to the agnostic, not to the scientist, to say otherwise. It is not impossible that a logician might proclaim that there is no logical contradiction to hold that the reverse is true, that perhaps it was the reindeers who drew the pictures. The remarkable thing is that no one would pay any attention to the logician, least of all the logician himself; that sort of logic is boring and unproductive. It may be that the logician, or the scientist, sees only a difference of degree, not in kind, between the man and the reindeer, that, from his point of view, the difference provides no justification for speaking of the human spirit, that what is found on the walls of a prehistoric cave proves nothing about anything. The point is that no sane person is going to pay any attention to such "Wonderland" logic. Nor will the sane person need to be very intelligent—certainly not very "intellectual"—to see the point.

Presumably what makes the primitive artist want to draw pictures of reindeer on the walls of his cave rather strongly resembles what makes the artist in any age want to sing or dance, write poetry or compose music, paint pictures or carve statues. There is, so it would seem, the human sense of wonder at the glories of creation, followed, at whatever great distance in time we do not know, by the self-conscious human awareness of a capacity to create in imitation of the luxurious wonders of creation. It might well be going beyond our capacity to know to say that primitive humans had an awareness of their being images of God, or even to guess when that awareness came, but we can certainly say that, if we have been created in the image of God, so were they. We can also say, without any serious fear of contradiction, that working out that image in the activity of creative productivity is the human mode of imaging God. Of all this, Chesterton was immeasurably aware. One has the impression that he was constantly being overwhelmed by the wonders of the world and by the wonders of human creativity; the response that both wonders called forth from him was, as we have already seen, the response of gratitude.

Here, however, it is important to make a significant distinction between thankfulness–for and thankfulness–to. There can be no question that Chesterton was constantly thankful for the wonders of nature, from the sunrise to the white cliffs of Dover, from the wonder of having two legs to walk with to the wonder of having the nightingale to listen to. But he was never thankful *to* nature, especially not when it was spelled with a capital N: Nature in that sense was for him only a metaphor, not a giver of gifts. From the standpoint of sheer rationality, Chesterton, who was simply thankful for so much, needed a personal Being *to* whom he could be thankful, and there began the pilgrimage to the God who was always beckoning him through generosity. What he could not stand was the dreariness of the naturalistic mind, which could look at the glories of nature and simply find that it couldn't be otherwise, for which the grass had to be green because it could not be otherwise: "Now the fairy-tale philosopher is glad that the leaf is green precisely because it might have been scarlet. He feels as if it had turned green an instant before he looked at it. He is pleased that the snow is white on the strictly reasonable ground that it might have been black."[21] As Chesterton saw it, reason itself *had* to see the whole of nature, not as something that had *happened*, but as something that had been *done*,[22] and thus it is reason that tells us that we must be grateful *to* the doer *for* the doing.

For the first thing the casual critic will say is "What nonsense all this is; do you mean that a poet cannot be thankful for grass and wild flowers without connecting it with theology; let alone your theology?" To which I answer, "Yes; I mean he cannot do it without connecting it with theology, unless he can do it without connecting it with thought. If he can manage to be thankful when there is nobody to be thankful to, and no good intentions to be thankful for, then he is simply taking refuge in being thoughtless in order to avoid being thankless." But indeed the argument goes beyond conscious gratitude, and applies to any sort of peace or confidence or repose, even unconscious confidence or repose. Even the nature-worship which Pagans have felt, even the nature-love which Pantheists have felt, ultimately depends as much on some implied purpose and positive good in things, as does the direct thanksgiving which Christians have felt. Indeed Nature is at best merely a female name we give to Providence when we are not treating it very seriously; a piece of feminist mythology. There is a sort of fireside fairytale, more fitted for the hearth than for the altar; and in that what is called Nature can be a sort of fairy godmother. But there can only be fairy godmothers because there are godmothers; and there can only be godmothers because there is God.[23]

The world is and is what it is because it is willed to be and to be what it is. We as human beings must be grateful to God that the world is and that we are. Even more, we must be grateful for the unique privilege we enjoy among earthly creatures of being able to be grateful. It is all very well to be amazed at the enormity of the gigantic solar system, but there is no reason to be cowed by it. "It is quite futile to argue that man is small compared to the cosmos, for man was always small compared to the nearest tree."[24] The cosmos, after all, is not made in the image and likeness of God; human beings are. Just as God, then, images himself outside himself in creation, so human artists—which all of us are in one way or another—are impelled to imitate God by putting themselves outside themselves in creating works of art, not, be it noted, for the sake of art, but for the sake of manifesting the wonder of being human.[25] In whatever the human imitator makes, we should be able to discover the human spirit. In proportion to our discovery of this will be the realization that life is more important than art; the latter is in the service of the former, not vice versa.

HUMAN CREATIVITY—FREEDOM

To say that human beings "make" things, in the sense of bringing into being what was not there before, is not to speak of what most specially characterizes human making. Spiders and ants, and bees and beavers, after all, make things that would not be there if they did not make them. What characterizes human creativity, like the divine creativity it images, is that it is the free activity of the subject acting. The science of Chesterton's day, like much of the science—particularly the "science" of human behavior—of our own day, was largely deterministic in its orientation. There is a certain contradiction here, but that does not seem to bother the determinists. This kind of scientist thinks in a deterministic rather than a humanistic way, because he or she prefers the kind of certainty science offers. To prefer, however, is to choose, and to choose is to choose freely, or it is nothing at all. We might, it is true, speak of a computer "choosing," but it is hardly likely that we should fail to recognize that this "choosing" is a metaphorical way of speaking of an operation—which the computer would not perform, if human beings had not freely chosen to construct an instrument that performs this operation. There is, it is true, no scientific "proof" of freedom; but that is not to say that there is no freedom; it is not even to say that it is not perfectly rational to *see* the reality of human freedom, where believing is seeing, and seeing is *knowing*. "Generally, the moral substance of liberty is this: that man is not meant merely to receive good laws, good food, or good conditions, but is meant to take a certain princely pleasure in selecting and shaping, like the gardener."[26] But it is precisely here that Chesterton and his opponents will never see eye-to-eye. To the kind of "scientific" mind in question, it makes no sense to say that man is "meant" to be or do anything. "Meant" means that *someone* does the meaning, and there is no one to do that; and to Chesterton it makes no sense to say that there is no one who does the *meaning*—"and never the twain shall meet." Now, it may very well be that determinism cannot be refuted by purely logical argument—no more than scepticism can—but the point at issue is not purely logical argument, it is life; neither the determinist nor the sceptic can consistently live that way. There need be no question that the very concept of free will, of a cause that produces effects freely and, therefore, unpredictably, is a paradox—but so is much else that is true.

One might, however, contend that one rejects this paradox only at the cost of accepting a much more unacceptable paradox. In *Orthodoxy*, Chesterton speaks of a controversy he was engaged in with the *Clarion* on the matter of free will, where "that able writer Mr. R. B. Suthers said that free will was lunacy, because it meant causeless actions, and the actions of a lunatic would be causeless."[27] Chesterton is quick to point out two not disparate paradoxes in this contention. (1) If any human actions, even those of a lunatic, are "causeless," then determinism cannot hold water, precisely because there *are* causeless actions. (2) It is precisely the actions of a lunatic that are *not* causeless; the lunatic has no choice. Later on, in the same *Orthodoxy*, Chesterton points out that the determinist has no right to any emotions, a highly inhuman way of behaving: "But it is a much more massive and important fact that he is not free to praise, to curse, to thank, to justify, to urge, to punish, to resist temptations, to incite mobs, to make New Year resolutions, to pardon sinners, to rebuke tyrants, or even to say 'thank you' for the mustard"[28]—a rather snail-like existence at best! Over against all this it is Chesterton's contention that freedom is indeed the first of God's gifts to human beings—even though a mighty risky gift. It is freedom that makes for the dignity of the human, but it is freedom too that makes for the possibility of sin. There is no way we can proclaim the worthwhileness of life by proclaiming the non-existence of evil; it is too obviously real and omnipresent. Nor does it solve anything to say that evil is simply an inevitable concomitant of existence: that eliminates the possibility of doing anything about it, and is eventually a surrender to pessimism. If, however, we can see that we humans have misused a good world and have not merely been entrapped in a bad one, which means that evil is the result of a wrong use of free will and can, thus, be righted by a right use of it, we shall be able to see that, even if free will is misused, it is better to have it than not to have it.[29]

One cannot, of course, believe in the reality of free choice and not believe that the past could have been other than it was. It is also freedom, however, that makes for the possibility of history—a completely determined series of events would not be history; it would be fiction. There is "history" in any intelligible sense of that term, only if what has happened *could* have been otherwise. "Nobody can prove or disprove it metaphysically; but I am the more content with a philosophy which permits of occasional miracles, because the alternative philosophy does not even permit of alternatives. It forbids a man even to dream of anything so natural as the Ifs of history."[30] What if, for example, in the course of history other decisions had been made by fallible human beings? By the same token it is worse than fictional to present progress as inevitable—the history of the world from 1914 to the present makes it simply impossible to believe that. There has, it is true, been abundant material progress, if that can

even be called progress when its by-products are so devastating, but there has been undeniable spiritual retrogression. If, however, we can see that history *could* have been
otherwise than it has been, we shall also be able to see
that the future can be different from what the present
seems to predict. "One of the most necessary and most
neglected points about the story called history is the fact
that the story is not finished."[31] We have to be able, as
Chesterton says, to "unthink the past,"[32] if we are to have
hope for the future. What is more difficult, however, is to
unthink the present. "We must realize that, in the mind
at least, Athens might never have been built, the Jews
might have been exterminated in the first fight with the
Canaanites, all Europe might have become Moslem or no
civilization existed except the Chinese. I am sure that the
right way to the realization of history is through this sort
of imaginative destruction; but when it comes to the case
before me, and I consider that it is ourselves and all our
own history that has thus to be imaginatively destroyed,
I despair."[33] Rare emotion for G. K. Chesterton, indeed!
It is perhaps for this reason that he eventually turned to
the Roman Catholic Church, which he found to be pre-
eminently on the side of freedom, not of fatalism, and
therefore on the side of hope. "Wherever that message [of
liberty] is heard, men think and talk in terms of will and
choice; and they see no meaning in any of the philosophies
of fate, whether desperate or resigned."[34]

It can seem strange, even to a Catholic, to find Chesterton so often and so strongly associating the teaching of
the Catholic Church with the advocacy of freedom, especially freedom of thought. If, however, we remind ourselves that he chose as his favorite adversaries certain
scientists with their advocacy of determinism and the
Calvinists with their advocacy of predestinationism, we
can understand how he experienced Catholic teaching as

a breath of fresh air. In his earlier days, of course, the days of *Heretics, Orthodoxy, What's Wrong with the World, A Short History of England,* and *Irish Impressions,* to mention but a few, he speaks simply of "Christianity," but after his conversion to Catholicism in 1922 he begins to speak of the Roman Church and the Roman tradition of England as embodying the authentic essence of Christianity itself. So true is this that in *The Everlasting Man* (1925) and thereafter he is constantly engaged in a defense of dogma, precisely as a liberating force, in the sense that it provides a spiritual center around which freedom of thought can gravitate. If we recollect that he found his way into the Catholic Church by freely thinking things out on his own, then finding in the teaching of the Catholic Church what he was convinced of already—and we can document that in his writings from the beginning—his views on dogma as a liberating force will not seem so very strange.

Perhaps what makes this more understandable is his constant insistence on a truth that should be obvious but is not always recognized as such—namely, that freedom is authentic only if it is *not* absolute. (One is reminded, incidentally, that Hegel, whom Chesterton neither knew nor appreciated, spoke to this most trenchantly in his *Phenomenology of Spirit,* Chapter VI, Section B, III, entitled "Absolute Freedom and the Terror," which could have been called "Anarchy and Chaos.") The point is that, when human spirit is at its freest, it makes laws and rules and institutions for itself and thus binds itself, realizing that to choose at all is to close the door on what the choosing excludes, which in the long run means that one makes oneself more authentically free by binding oneself. "We are never free until some institution frees us."[35] He sees the Catholic Church performing precisely this function of liberation.

Putting aside the strict sense of a Catholic courage, the world ought to be told something about Catholic intellectual independence. It is, of course, the one quality which the world supposes that Catholics have lost. It is also, at this moment, the one quality which Catholics perceive that all the world has lost. The modern world has many marks, good as well as bad; but by far the most modern thing in it is the abandonment of individual reason, in favour of press stunts and suggestion and mass psychology and mass production. The Catholic Faith, which always preserves the unfashionable virtue, is at this moment alone sustaining the independent intellect of man.[36]

The only freedom that is authentic is limited freedom, the freedom that limits itself. Chesterton illustrates this by commenting on the omnipresence of "walls" in the medieval Catholic design of things, in its landscape, its architecture, its heraldry, its stained glass, its painting.[37] Even its prohibitions in the long run promote reason and liberty.[38] It is worth noting that a good many British converts to Catholicism have been drawn to it by its capacity to define authoritatively what is to be believed, thus freeing the human spirit of its own arbitrariness. What Chesterton unfortunately does not say—converts, especially British converts, seldom do—is that not everything that is called "Catholic teaching" necessarily is so. What it comes down to is that there can be meaningful disagreement only where there is agreement on principles. "But wherever the falsity appears it comes from neglect of the same truth: that men should agree on a principle, that they may differ on everything else; that God gave men a law that they might turn it into liberties."[39]

There is, it must be admitted, a certain risk of ambiguity or vagueness in employing language about freedom, precisely because very clear distinctions of meaning are imperative, and the modern mind tends to be impatient with fine distinctions. Take, for example, the proud American boast that the Constitution guarantees "freedom of religion." So it does, and one of the safeguards of this freedom has been thought to be found in the principle of separation of Church and State, in the sense that the establishment by the State of one Church would impede human freedom in religious matters, as it did, for example, in England and in Spain. What was originally intended, however, as a guarantee either that religious bodies would exist freely or that individuals would be free *to* engage in a variety of religious practices has become in the contemporary secularist mind a freedom *from* religion. By the same token, freedom *for*, which is clearly a means to an end beyond merely being free, has become in the modern mind a freedom *to* act, such that the free action is an end in itself and not a quality to be used in the creation of what is beyond itself. It may well be that the freedom to make mistakes is a necessary condition for the freedom to bring about what is good, but the good brought about is the end aimed at by the action, what the action is *for*—purposeless action is not free, it is random. Much has been said also about freedom of speech and freedom of the press, but if all these freedoms consist in concretely is the freedom to talk or write and not the freedom to determine our own lives—a rather rare privilege under the domination of modern plutocracy—freedom of speech and freedom of the press are rather empty freedoms indeed. On the other hand, even the freedom to determine our own lives is a freedom which can be exercised only within reasonable limits, and perhaps freedom of speech and of the press could, if they were real freedoms, promote an understanding of what reasonable limits are. Freedom in this sense is, at the very least, limited by the freedom of others. It may be that, strictly speaking, we cannot logically prove that liberty is a good thing—especially to those who, in one way or another, *prefer* not to be free, or not to let others be free— but it is unquestionably true that to lose one's belief in liberty is to lose one's belief in humanity, which certainly makes a difference and is a very bad thing.

There is, we can suppose, a certain logic behind the contention that freedom of spirit is incompatible with absolutely unalterable laws of nature. There might even be a logic in the contention that there can be no completely scientific comprehension of reality, if the laws that govern reality are not unalterable. There is no logic at all in the contention that there can be no nature at all, unless its laws are unalterable, or that the co-called incompatibility of freedom and nature has to be solved in favor of nature. Chesterton was very much aware that the modern emphasis on nature runs the risk of dehumanizing the human in either or both of two ways: (1) by making human existence natural and only natural—the supposition apparently being that to spell Nature with a capital N is to make it coterminous with the whole of reality; and (2) by subordinating the human individual to Nature—again spelled with a capital—such that the function of the human is to serve nature, and not vice versa.[40] It is doubtful, of course, that sound common sense would give the time of day to such nonsense, but it is also doubtful that anyone who thinks along these lines would give the time of day to common sense—"common," after all, is synonymous with "vulgar"! What lies behind this attitude of what can be called a "rationalistic elite" is, it would seem, a fear, fear of the supernatural, as though to believe in it would somehow threaten human dignity. Here we should have to admit that "Naturalism" has won a number of skirmishes in its ongoing battle for control of the human mind. It must also be said, however, that the mind of G. K. Chesterton contributed mightily to the struggle against the naturalistic superstition in the first three decades of this century. He did so, not by downgrading nature, but, so to speak, by upgrading nature, seeing in it a colossal manifestation of supernature, an enduring proclamation of the greatness of God. At the same time, it should be noted, he saw in nature an enduring proclamation of the greatness of the human spirit, in the sense both that the proclamation is made to the human spirit only and that the human spirit in its contemplation of nature becomes aware of its own greatness, i.e., its capacity to transform nature in order to satisfy the demands of Spirit. When we say that, *The Everlasting Man* immediately comes to mind, but the theme is a constant in all that Chesterton wrote.

No one, it is true, is completely devoid of prejudices; to believe strongly is, in a sense, to engage in a prejudice against the opposite of what one believes. In this sense, Chesterton, too, was prejudiced—and he was aware of it. At the same time, he was extraordinarily sensitive to the prejudices of others, especially of those who thought they were not prejudiced. He was keenly aware, for example, that disbelief itself was a form of faith, a faith in the all-sufficiency of matter to explain itself, to lift itself by its own bootstraps, and thus to transform itself into life, and thought, and artistic creativity—and this faith, this disbelief, is propounded dogmatically, as though it is not possible for reason to doubt it.[41] To believe that the material nature that develops in so many ways is created by a personal divine spiritual being is considered arbitrary, whereas it is not considered arbitrary to claim that infinite time is an adequate ground for all the development that has taken place, including the very existence of what develops. There are, Chesterton would tell us, no grounds for believing that the slowness of a process of change makes the process in question more natural, in any significant sense of that term, and more intelligible. In itself the pace of a process has nothing to do with the reason for it.[42] There are, it would seem, no limits to the credulity of materialist dogmatism, nor are there limits to the claim that those who propose infinite spirit as the source of all existence are the ones who are dogmatic.[43] Materialism is a creed, a *dogmatic* creed, which holds to the abstract principle of the impossibility of creation or miracle.[44] Nowhere, incidentally, do we find Chesterton denying that expectation of divine intervention or miracle *can* be superstition—especially where the religion in question is paganism. The point, however, is that such expectation (or hope, or desire) is not *a priori* superstitious. One gets the impression, on the other hand, that frequently those who deny the divine or the miraculous do so, not so much because they think they have proved that the divine or the miraculous is impossible, but much more because they are convinced that divine intervention is *undesirable.* It is this that characterizes the thought of a Marx, a Feuerbach, a Nietzsche, or a Sartre.[45] One also gets the impression that, just as Chesterton came to belief in God, in Christianity, and ultimately in the Catholic Church, because he wanted to thank someone for the marvelous world in which he lived and for the marvelous privilege of being human, so those who fought the divine origin of the natural and the supernatural origin of the human did so because they did not want to be thankful, because they somehow found thankfulness degrading. This last is clearly true of the four anti-theists we have mentioned. It is not easy to argue with such men, since their mind is made up, and their emotions are unalterable. It is not at all difficult to see, however, that not one of them is more rational than Chesterton, if, of course, rationality is in question at all. This brings us, it would seem, to what we might call the supremely rational thought of Chesterton the social idealist.

———◆———

The manuscript of this study had already been completed and submitted for publication when there came into my hands a recent book with the unlikely and fascinating title *Chesterton, a Seer of Science*.[46] The author, Stanley Jaki, is well known as both a historian and a philosopher of science, but that fact does not prepare one for the connection he makes between Chesterton and science in the contemporary sense of that term. But the mystery does not stop there: in the very first chapter, "Interpreter of Science," Jaki notes with a sense of bafflement that biographers of and commentators on Chesterton are universally silent about the significance of his thought to the scientific endeavor, whereas in 1957 Martin Gardner, associate editor of *American Scientist*, who had no sympathy whatever with Chesterton's metaphysics, included a selection from Chapter 4 of Chesterton's *Orthodoxy* (1908), "The Ethics of Elfland," in a volume entitled *Great Essays in Science*. This put Chesterton in company with such scientific giants as Albert Einstein, Charles Darwin, Henri Fabre, J. R. Oppenheimer, Arthur Stanley Eddington, and Alfred North Whitehead, to say nothing of prominent interpreters of science like John Dewey, Ernest Nagel, and the Huxleys.

Perhaps the answer to the riddle is contained in the term "seer," which claims neither that Chesterton was a scientist nor one who knew enough science to be able to criticize its practitioners. What it does claim is that Chesterton was endowed with the sort of prophetic wisdom that enabled him to reflect on scientific reasoning, especially in its pseudo-scientific forms of "scientism," "evolutionism," "eugenics," and "materialistic determinism." What can be said is that Chesterton was consistently critical of the unmetaphysical metaphysics of those scientists who failed to discern the limits of the legitimate application of the scientific method, thus drawing unscientific conclusions for which they could give no evidence. What all this means is, perhaps, best summed up in the remark made by Martin Gardner in his introduction to the Chesterton selection in *Great Essays*, quoted by Jaki: "The rotund British writer was not noted for his knowledge of things scientific. . . . Yet there are times, as in the following selection, when he startles you with unexpected scientific insights."[47] It is to be hoped that the present chapter bears out what Gardner says here and what Jaki seeks to drive home throughout his book.

5

Social Thought

ONE OF THE REASONS why Chesterton, despite his obvious writing talent, could not abandon journalism and concentrate his efforts on literary creativity was his constant concern for people in the concrete. This meant, of course, not only a profound interest in each and every individual with whom he came in contact, but also and more significantly an awareness of and concern with the larger framework within which human beings live their lives. As we have already noted, moral values never relinquished their claim on Chesterton's attention, but moral values cannot be realized in a vacuum; they are no more than merely abstract apart from the religious, social, political, and economic dimensions of life as it is lived. Only if we are constantly aware of these four dimensions of Chesterton's concern will we be able to come to grips with his thought, which he expresses in a language that is both allusive and elusive. The point, however, is, as we have already seen, that Chesterton's conviction of the responsibility of art—and of the artist—to society made him far more concerned with the content of what he had to say than with the literary form in which he said it, even though the form of his writing made the content so striking.

What characterized Chesterton throughout his life, after he had passed through a youthful hyper-intellectual agnosticism, was an extraordinary sense of the sacredness, the awesomeness of simply being human. It was not that he loved "all men"—the rather amorphous mass of humanity, the object of the philanthropist's love—but that he found human beings lovable as he met them in the concrete, which most of us, quite frankly, simply do not do. No one, of course, could find everyone equally lovable—that would in itself be inhuman—but if anyone was able to find each and every human being wonderful, that man was Chesterton. What is more, it was precisely what is ordinary in each human being that, for Chesterton, made them all in a significant way lovable. His sense of democracy was not simply an abstract political doctrine of equal rights; it was the concrete conviction that every human being is of equal dignity—that it was this "equal dignity" that was "ordinary" about them. "The sense of the miracle of humanity itself should be always more vivid to us than any marvels of power, intellect, art, or civilization. The mere man on two legs, as such, should be felt as something more heartbreaking than any music and more startling than any caricature."[1] As we have had to note before, almost everything Chesterton wrote was autobiographical. We can see this in what he says of Charles Dickens: "There is a great man who makes every man feel small. But the real great man is the man who makes every man feel great."[2] It may be that this last remark was not exactly true of Charles Dickens of whom he said it, but it certainly was true of Gilbert Chesterton himself. Over and over again, those who knew Chesterton during his lifetime testify to the extraordinary capacity he had in conversation to make others feel that they were being brilliant. He was simply convinced that there is a greatness to everybody—and he had a very special gift for bringing that greatness out. The conviction, however, was essentially a religious conviction, the conviction that all of us are "made in the image and likeness of God," that greatness is God's gift to those he made human, and that what he himself had to give to those same humans was making them aware of precisely that. In this connection it might seem that Chesterton was speaking with tongue in cheek when he calls himself simply "ordinary," but there can be little doubt that he really meant that—he was, in fact, extraordinarily ordinary, because he held with extraordinary vigor to what we might call ordinary values, or the value of being ordinary. "I am ordinary in the correct sense of the term, which means the acceptance of an order, a Creator and the Creation, the common sense of gratitude for Creation, life and love as gifts permanently good, marriage and chivalry as laws rightly controlling them, and the rest of the normal traditions of our race and religion."[3] It is most important to stress the very last word in that quote; the equality of all is not a merely rational truth—in fact, mere reason could never come to grips with it—it is a religious truth; we are all equal because God created us all, because we are all equally children of God, because God loves us all. To speak of equality without a Creator is not to speak rationally at all. "Jefferson said that men were given equal rights by their Creator. Ingersoll said they had no Creator, but had received equal rights from nowhere."[4] There is, it is clear, a certain lack of logic in wanting to hold on to a democratic affirmation of equality while denying the only possible source of that equality: unless, of course, the affirmation comes not from rational conviction so much as from emotional preference. "There is no basis for democracy except in a dogma about the divine origin of man. That is a perfectly simple fact which the modern world will find out more and more to be a fact. Every other basis is a sort of sentimental confusion, full of merely verbal echoes of the older creeds."[5] One has to wonder, of course, how many self-styled "democrats" really do believe in universal human equality in any but an abstractly political sense. It would seem that at both extremes of the ideological scale—the capitalistic and the socialistic—equality is but an emotional catchword, to which reality does not correspond, unless, of course, what is meant by "equal" is equally insignificant, equally despicable, equally vile. Perhaps the best way to characterize Chesterton's attitude is as a special kind of reverence before the divine image in each human being, not merely in those beings who are at the top of the plutocratic or bureaucratic ladder. One thing is certain: only the community of the divine image in all humans can make talk about "equality" more than a mockery. It is the sort of attitude that reaches its highest pitch in a saint like Francis of Assisi, about whom Chesterton wrote so eloquently, precisely because Francis was for him both hero and ideal. It is not without significance that, when Chesterton looked for one term to express this attitude as he saw it in Francis, what he found was the term "courtesy," expressing as he saw it a "moral and religious idea,"[6] which takes it out of the drawing rooms of the aristocracy into the highways and byways of the world. Of this spirit which Francis exemplified so strikingly, Chesterton himself imbibed deeply. Only if we understand this will we know what it means to speak of Chesterton's unalterable devotion to democracy: "Democracy is not founded on pity for the common man; democracy is founded on reverence for the common man, or, if you will, even on fear of him. It does not champion man because man is so miserable, but because man is so sublime."[7] This, by the way, is not equivalent to the Franciscan love of all human beings; it is simply the presumption of equality that is the prerequisite to love.[8] It may be that to see the divine image in each human being demands a supernatural insight, but given that insight the love following it is quite intelligible—at least to a Chesterton, as to a Francis. That Francis also loved animals does not mean that the love in question was the same in both cases. To which we might add that loving all human beings is not loving all their opinions, no more than saying that all are equals is the same as saying that all their opinions are equally true.

There can be little doubt that, when Chesterton speaks about "democracy" and "equality," he is contrasting it chiefly with "aristocracy" as he experienced it in the Britain of his day. The point he is trying to make, however, has at most an indirect relationship to the question of focus on government. What he has in mind is the equality of one human being with another simply from the fact that both are human beings, such that nothing added to the dignity of humanness can be a reason for one being justifiably considered superior to another, *qua* human being. There is no reason to question incidental superiorities. Some people are unquestionably more intelligent than others, some more artistic, more scientific, more athletic; some are better writers, better poets, better teachers, even better politicians. But there are no different "kinds" of human beings, such that by nature one "kind" is better than another—not by race, not by sex, not by color. No one has a "natural right" to dominate over others—*pace* Nietzsche. In this sense all of us are equally "ordinary"; each of us is "the common man"—or "woman." There are doubtless those who surpass others in their accomplishments, but it is precisely their accomplishments that become the common property of the human family. It may take a little juggling on our part to come to terms with what Chesterton means by "common," but until we do we shall fail to understand anything else he says, particularly when he is speaking in political terms.

> But with this mere phrase, the common mind, we collide with a current error. Commonness and the common mind are now generally spoken of as meaning in some manner inferiority and the inferior mind; the mind of the mere mob.

But the common mind means the mind of all artists and heroes; or else it would not be common. Plato had the common mind; Dante had the common mind; or that mind was not common. Commonness means the quality common to the saint and the sinner, to the philosopher and the fool.[9]

There can be no question that what Chesterton means by "common" particularly when connected with "sense" or "mind" does not have the meaning it is *commonly* held to have, nor is it quite clear that he is not being somewhat inventive in his use of the term; in any event, he does equate "common" sense with good sense. If, then, what he is trying to get across is that ordinary people— whoever they are—are better guides where values are concerned than are a self-appointed elite, he is at least proposing a thesis which stands a chance of being for the most part correct. If, in addition, he is more concerned with tantalizing us into thinking for ourselves than with being merely "correct," what he has to say may very well turn out to be quite worthwhile. It remains true, however, that Chesterton not infrequently simply identifies "the common mind," "common sense," and "common opinion" with what he himself, after profound reflection, considers to be true—and, more often than not, what he calls "common" is not only eminently worth listening to but also eminently *uncommon* in the accepted sense. Sometimes, of course, we have to do a little interpreting, if we are to make good sense of what Chesterton says. Thus, when he says: "Fiction means the common things as seen by the uncommon people. Fairy tales mean the uncommon things as seen by the common people,"[10] we may have to change the last phrase into "by people seeing in common" to get the full import of what he is saying: i.e., the "commonness" of which he speaks is that "quality common to the saint and the sinner, to the philosopher and the fool."[11]

It may be that we shall see better the full thrust of what Chesterton has to say about equality, democracy, and justice, if we understand his conviction that the coexistence of great wealth and great poverty among a people in the concrete makes equality and, thus, truth an impossible dream. This, of course, amounts to the conviction that democracy never did, in fact, take root in Britain—which does not imply pinning any roses on American democracy.[12] Still, what he did see in his own Britain, from the eighteenth to the twentieth centuries, was the rich becoming constantly richer and the poor constantly poorer, with the result that equality of rights was not a reality, and self-government by the British people was simply not achieved—plutocracy was. Here it is that Chesterton the idealist pleads with all of us not to give up hope. Even if democracy has in fact failed, that is no reason to cease believing in it as a realizable ideal, no reason to give in to the cynicism of accepting without hope the domination of a wealthy elite, even if it be an elected elite. "If democracy has disappointed you, do not think of it as a burst bubble, but at least as a broken heart, an old love-affair. Do not sneer at the time when the creed of humanity was on its honeymoon; treat it with the dreadful reverence that is due to youth."[13] It is significant that, although Chesterton's early sympathy for Socialism—especially in the form of "Christian Socialism"—never completely disappeared, it was very clear to him that Communism (or any form of collectivism) was just as undemocratic as capitalism,[14] just as unable to trust "ordinary" people to govern themselves, and thus needing to impose itself on those who do not freely choose it. No *people* has ever freely chosen Communism (with a capital C).

There is nothing wrong with democracy; there is nothing wrong with the people ruling, except what is wrong with anybody out of the people ruling; what is wrong is forgetting that people are only people. They will make mistakes, as you and I make mistakes; and as all our superiors, the supermen, the dictators, the makers of modern systems, will also make them. There was only one supreme modern mistake, which was that men forgot for a hundred years that they are liable to make mistakes.[15]

Almost thirty years before, in *Orthodoxy*, Chesterton had put it very succinctly: "In short, the democratic faith is this: the most terribly important things must be left to ordinary men themselves—the mating of the sexes, the rearing of the young, the laws of the state."[16]

LOVE OF THE POOR

Chesterton's unremitting advocacy of the authentic ideal of democracy—an ideal unrealized where either wealth and power or bureaucracy and power are coterminous— is inseparable from his personal love for and sympathy with the poor. For him there was no such thing as the problem of poverty, even though he was quite aware of a causal connection between the greediness of the rich and the poverty of the poor; his concern was with poor human beings, who by right were in every way equal to the rich, but who in modern society were treated as inferior in every way. His desire was not that the poor should become rich; his desire was that the poor should be happy. Cure poverty, yes, but not at the expense of negating "Blessed are the poor." Make conditions better for the poor, yes, but, better still, give the poor the opportunity to better their own conditions by their own efforts. If there is one thing the poor do not need, however, it is pity, which is but one remove from contempt. Reform is needed, to be sure, but it is not the poor who need to be reformed; what needs to be reformed is the society that in satisfying the greed of the rich fails to satisfy the need of the poor. It might be argued, of course, that many of the abuses Chesterton so eloquently scored have since been remedied and that, thus, his attacks need no longer be taken seriously. The principles he enunciated, however, continue to be valid, and it would be utterly naïve to think that the inequalities, the injustices he excoriated have simply vanished. The "system" continues to be a failure, and if Chesterton were around today, he would continue to say so. It might also be said that, in the concrete, individuals and even groups can do so little about the situation. Manufacturers still produce "goods" to sell to people and thus to make money—lots of it. The making of money is clearly the main reason for making what is made, and this means persuading people to buy what is made, even when it is not needed or, worse still, not *good* for them. The point, however, is that G. K. Chesterton can still speak powerfully to our consciences, and the conscience his words are directed to is the conscience of humanity. It may be said that Chesterton's fight for the poor was, in fact, ineffective; it is still true that his words were in some way prophetic. In the words of T. S. Eliot in his obituary of Chesterton: "Even if Chesterton's social and political ideas appear totally without effect . . . are demonstrated wrong . . . they were the ideas for his time that were fundamentally Christian. . . . He did more than any man of his time . . . to maintain the existence of the important minority in the modern world"[17]—the "important minority," of course, being authentic Christians. We today can look back at Britain's "poor laws" and see in them a terrible legal travesty, but how many were there who fought them with the vigor—and even the effectiveness—of Chesterton? Nor should we forget that the principles that underlay his fighting constituted his "philosophy." It may be that the professional philanthropists—who loved humanity but not human beings—who were responsible for laws of this type, were trying to help the poor, but Chesterton saw clearly that this sort of tyrannical paternalism was not the way to do it; bureaucratic regulation of the lives of the poor serves only to humiliate them, not to help them. Helping the poor at the cost of their personal liberty and privacy is depriving them of their dignity as human beings. Chesterton went so far as to condemn the evil of compulsory education, which to us in America might seem, in light of our own public school system, to be going too far. What he was against, however, was taking education out of the parents' hands altogether, "taking children out of their homes in order to teach them to despise everything their parents thought and felt."[18] One wonders if the advocates of compulsory education were terribly concerned to improve relations between parents and children. What they in fact accomplished was to alienate parents and children from each other. Chesterton saw as well as anyone that adequate education was indispensable to the maintenance of dignity, but he also saw that bureaucratic control was the enemy of dignity.

Chesterton was certainly not unaware that, in practically any country in the world, the crime rate among the very poor will at least seem to be higher than in any other group in society. The reasons given for this, of course, can range from the claim that the state of poverty induces crime, which might cause one to ask why there are still such enormous numbers of the poor who do not commit crimes, even when they are destitute, to the more concrete claim that the poor are much more likely to be caught and successfully prosecuted than are those belonging to other levels of society, which claim does not quite explain enough. Chesterton simply does not attempt either to explain or to explain away the claims; what he does is to highlight the self-respect, the honor, dignity, pride, and triumph that is so often witnessed among the poor, often enough to demolish any *a priori* expectation that poverty and crime will be inevitably linked: except, of course, in a capitalist culture where poverty itself—or even the absence of a desire simply to "make money," to "have ambition," in the crassest sense of that term—is looked upon as some sort of moral fault. He was also very much aware of the crimes of the well-to-do. There is another aspect of this question, which Chesterton brings out poignantly in his book on William Cobbett, where he speaks of a sense of "honor" that was shared by Cobbett and the young servant girl he was eventually to marry. "It is something seldom understood in a society without peasants; an oligarchy which can only understand what we call 'honour' as it is understood by gentlemen. It was the self-respect of the poor, which all modern industrial society has been slowly crushing to death."[19] It is admittedly not easy in our modern world to respect the humanity of "vulgar," "shabby," and "ignorant" people. It is difficult, too, to refuse to be impressed by wealth and cleverness. Perhaps it takes a special kind of virtue and insight, with which G. K. Chesterton was so generously endowed, to recognize that being fit to perform excellently any number of non-moral functions and being a misfit at being human are not necessarily incompatible. It might not be going too far to call Chesterton an outstanding champion of unfashionable values in a world where it was more important to be fashionable than it was to be *true*, in the double sense of true to oneself and true in one's opinions.

Much of what we might call Chesterton's constant campaigning for the poor was guided by his fierce opposition to what today, in light of the Nazi travesty, we have to call the insanely misguided "science" of "eugenics." In a capitalist society, where heaping up wealth is the equivalent of heroic virtue, those who fail to do so are readily looked upon as either unfit or perverse. One way of working out the implications of this worship of wealth is to control the breeding of offspring, a process that has proved enormously successful—and rewarding—in the case of race horses, dogs, cows, and pigs. That some "scientist" should get the idea that this sort of thing would be desirable among human beings is perhaps natural among those who see a human being as only a special kind of animal. "Scientific" breeding of human beings, however, runs up against what have to be called insuperable obstacles. There are experts among human beings both in knowing how to breed race horses, dogs, cows, and prize pigs and in knowing what it is desirable to breed in such animals, making them "fit" for what they ought to do—i.e., in what human beings desire them to do. When it comes to human beings, on the other hand, it is not too likely that we shall know either what kind of breeding will make them either fit or unfit or what it is desirable that they be fit for. Now, as Chesterton saw it, the British version of "eugenics"—which was not of the Nazi "Superman" variety—was more negative than positive; it did not quite know what fitness meant, but it did claim to know what unfitness meant, and it found the latter primarily among the poor. Its task was not so much to promote fitness, a rather nebulous task, but to prevent unfitness, a rather arbitrary prejudice.

There is, of course, another very serious danger inherent in any theory of selective breeding, which Chesterton effectively caricatures under the heading not of eugenics but of evolution. It is a question of the possibility of developing human types that will prove to be useful for the purposes of the powerful—which is to say, types who will submit to the oppression that makes them useful instruments on an assembly-line: "it will offer to breed slaves; to produce a new race indifferent to its rights."[20] There is a very subtle point here, and its significance needs to be emphasized. If it is possible to breed human beings in such a way that they cease to be aware of being oppressed, a new class of slaves will have been developed, completely under the domination of their masters. Only a *belief* in the divinity of the human, of the inviolability of the human ideal, will effectively prevent this: "Unless we have some doctrine of a divine man, all abuses may be excused, since evolution may turn them into uses. It will be easy for the scientific plutocrat to maintain that humanity will adapt itself to any conditions which we now consider evil."[21] The picture may be derived from nineteenth-century Britain, but, *mutatis mutandis*, it describes a situation that is still all too familiar. It was not all that easy to see in Chesterton's day how different a factory really is from a prison.[22] It is still a question whether it is possible to become exceedingly rich without oppressing those who make the accumulation possible, nor does the naïve theory of Adam Smith that what brings profit to the rich ultimately benefits the whole society help to answer the question.

It should not be without significance to point out in this connection, what Ian Boyd has brought out so well in his book *The Novels of G. K. Chesterton*, that the novels consistently express the social and political thought of their author and that the characters in them are not, strictly speaking, individuals but types, representing social and political ideas.[23] There is a sense in which social criticism was never completely absent from anything Chesterton wrote; it was his conviction that society as constituted was unjust, and he rarely let pass the chance to say so. By no stretch of the imagination could he agree with those who would look upon the sad state of society as inevitable or irremediable. He was, however, very realistic in his views of the actual situation and very much aware of the difficulty of remedying it, given the power of plutocracy to perpetuate itself. In this connection it should be emphasized that when Chesterton speaks, as he so often does, of "materialism," he is not speaking of some abstract metaphysical theory regarding the structure of reality—he is not, in fact, speaking of a "theory" at all; he is speaking of a value-attitude that characterizes so much of contemporary culture, of seeing in material values, things, satisfactions, and comforts the primary goals of human striving. Even where in theory spiritual values take precedence, in practice contemporary culture makes it barely possible to avoid the reversal of values.

Although Chesterton held no doctorate and did not even attend a university, he was in another sense a superbly educated man—largely self-educated. One sign of education in this sense is the ability to appreciate what education is geared to do *to* and *for* the person being educated. Education in this sense should enable us to take a critical view of contemporary institutions, which does not necessarily mean a negative view but simply an informed view, which permits us to *judge* those institutions against the backdrop of ideals, models, traditions that express the accumulated wisdom of the human family. "The whole point of education is that it should give a man abstract and eternal standards, by which he can judge material and fugitive conditions. If the citizen is to be a reformer, he must start with some ideal which he does not obtain merely by gazing reverently at the unreformed institutions."[24] Among the institutions he is concerned with in this context, and was concerned with throughout his whole writing career, was the commercial institution, which dominated—and still dominates—the scene.

> Everybody ought to learn first a general view of the history of man, of the nature of man, and (as I, for one, should add)

of the nature of God. This may enable him to consider the rights and wrongs of slavery in a slave community, of cannibalism in a cannibal community, or of commerce in a commercial community. If he is immediately initiated into the mysteries of these institutions themselves, if he is sworn in infancy to take them as seriously as they take themselves, if he becomes a trader not only before he became a traveler, but even before he becomes a true citizen of his own town, he will never be able to denounce those institutions—or even to improve them.[25]

THE FAMILY

It may seem like some sort of unexplained, or unexplainable, leap to move rapidly from these reflections on social, political, and economic institutions to what Chesterton always considered the most fundamental—and most important—of all social institutions, the family. One of the most important concerns of Chesterton's thought and writing, however, is the authenticity of human growth and development. Apart from his constant insistence on the divine origin of all things in general and of human life in particular he devotes much of his attention to the part that human beings themselves play in carrying out the divine plan of creation. They do this, not as the animals do, by merely instinctive activities of procreation and nurture, but by consciously and freely choosing to act in such a way as to achieve goals they set for themselves. What is essentially required for this is that man and woman come together to procreate and stay together to nurture and educate—which means seeing marriage and the family as the most basic form of society. The most basic form of society, however, is not adequate to the fulfillment of all its own needs: the religious needs of human relationship to God, the spiritual needs of mental and moral growth, the material needs of survival and satisfaction. To supply all the needs that human beings have, the basic familial societies must unite to form larger and larger, more and more complex societies. All of this must necessarily be, if the human race is to survive. But, as Chesterton sees it, there is a catch. With growth in size and complexity there comes into existence the super-society, the state, which ultimately subordinates to itself all other social groupings and, in so doing, more and more imperiously regulates their functioning. Instead of the state being, as it should be, the servant of the people, the people have become servants of the state. There is an obvious exaggeration in this last—except, perhaps, when what is in question is the totalitarian state—since the sum-total of the people constitute the state, but Chesterton was reacting to the very concrete situation in which the people, in fact, have less and less to say as to the functioning of the state, and the government of the state has more and more to say about the functioning of subordinate social groupings. It is all very well to say, in theory, that the people constitute the state; in contemporary society the people have precious little to say about the constitution of the state.

It is not strange, then, that Chesterton should have put so much emphasis on that society without which there would be no state, i.e., the family. For many, it is true, Chesterton will come across as too utterly intransigent on a number of issues: on the absolute indissolubility of marriage, for example, or on the prohibition of birth control, or on the undesirability of compulsory anything whatever, from education to health insurance; but we have to remember (1) that he was reacting to extremes that had developed in the first three decades of the twentieth century, and (2) that informed choice in many matters was becoming more and more difficult to achieve. Take divorce, for example. It might be argued that in extreme cases some provision should be made for rectifying mistakes that have been made, but it is scarcely conceivable that one-half of all marriages are extreme cases or that marriage is an essentially impermanent institution. It should at least be allowable to ask whether the enormous increase in the divorce rate—in the West, at any rate—is not undermining the foundations of society. It might also be asked quite seriously whether a union entered into under the antecedent conviction that it can readily be terminated is a marriage at all. "To be divorced is to be in the literal sense unmarried; and there is no sense in a thing being undone when we do not know if it is done."[26] It seems scarcely impolite for Chesterton to ask people just what they think they are doing when they marry. Nor would it be unreasonable to insist that the words uttered in the marriage ceremony express a *vow* of permanency.[27] For purely legal reasons the state may call marriage a "contract," but a Christian will call it a "sacrament"—or, at least, a "covenant"—which is not to be dissolved with the same ease as a contract. Perhaps the problem is not that the divorce rate is so high so much as that the marriage rate (among unions) is so low. One has to wonder whether a creeping cynicism in modern society with regard to the sacredness of any promise whatever makes it more and more difficult for people to make an informed choice in regard to the marriage *vow*—with its normal expectation of permanence. One has to wonder too whether the growing lack of fidelity to the small-scale society of the family will not issue in a corrosion of fidelity to the larger-scale society that exists for both the promotion and the betterment of human life.

There is, we have to admit, a sense in which Chesterton's interests were rather parochial. He could, it is true, write a book entitled *What's Wrong with the World*; and he could continually attack the evil he called "Prussianism" while praising what he called the "Republicanism" of the French; he could write about Rome, about Poland and Ireland and America; but his main concern always was what's wrong with Britain—which implied the question, "What must be done to make it better?" We have already seen a good deal of his social criticism, which tells us some of the answers to his questions. We have also seen his concern for the poor along with his conviction that the industrial structure of the society he lived in gave little hope of any improvement of the lot of the poor, which is to say of the vast majority of the working class in Britain. Industrial capitalism, he was convinced, had not only failed to better the lives of the vast majority of the British; it had produced and was continuing to produce the conditions that could only make the existence of the working-class poor worse than it already was. If we go back to the days of *Heretics* (1906) and *Orthodoxy* (1908), we shall be able to understand Chesterton's early sympathy with Socialism as an answer to the capitalist emphasis on wealth at any cost, which, as he saw it, inevitably implied the degradation of the poor workers who by their work made possible the accumulation of wealth in other hands than their own. In his notebooks of the previous decade, Maisie Ward tells us, Chesterton shows how he tried to come to grips intellectually with the conflicting strands of social thought vying with each other in his youth. Out of this, and after his conversion to Christianity, Chesterton begins to find that a Socialism imbued with the ideals of basic Christianity has the power to satisfy, if not his head, at least his heart. His emotions as a Christian cannot fail to vibrate with the protests of socialists against the inequalities which society as currently constituted, with its emphasis on competition, inevitably perpetuates. Ownership in common may not be the only answer, nor even the best answer, to selfish accumulation of wealth (Adam Smith's "enlightened self-interest"),[28] but it is better than no answer at all. Both Christianity and Socialism are opposed to the enormous accumulation of wealth in the hands of a tiny minority of the population, and, since what makes this accumulation possible is the exclusive possession of the means of production, Christianity and Socialism are again in agreement. They are also in agreement in seeking an effective remedy to the situation, but here Socialism would seem to have more clearcut plans for action.[29]

Chesterton's sympathy with Socialism, however, has its limitations, and those limitations are part and parcel of his Christian commitment. He himself was convinced that Socialism need not be atheistic, but he was also very much aware that the most systematic form of Socialism, i.e., Marxist Communism, is also systematically atheistic— out of a conviction that the only way human beings can effectively overcome oppression is to do it themselves, and that the only way to do it themselves is to do it without a God, especially a God who could seem to be favoring the rich; the ideal way to get rid of God is to concoct a silly God who could not exist, the silly God Marx invented. It is, in this connection, most interesting that Chesterton argues against atheistic Socialism not so much on religious as on humanistic grounds. Atheistic Socialism, he contends, will never be adopted by the common consent of a people, thinking autonomously, but only by way of imposition by state power, which would seem to be exactly what has happened. "That men may protest against law, it is necessary that they should believe in justice. That they may believe in a justice beyond law, it is necessary that they should believe in a justice beyond the land of living men. You can impose the rule of the Bolshevist as you can impose the rule of the Bourbons; but it is equally an imposition."[30] *A fortiori*, an atheism thus imposed will not be the atheism of people determining themselves freely. Still, even though he never ceases to oppose what he constantly calls "Bolshevist" socialism, he is far more concerned with attacking its opposite number, industrial capitalism, without which there never would have been any Communism. It is ironic that capitalism should be the product of "liberal economics," which is liberal only to the extent that it liberates the rich to get richer, with the result that the poor get poorer.[31] We might add that it is not without significance that a "liberal economics" which is not interested in freedom for all should pave the way for a system which, no matter how much Marx thought of it in the abstract as liberating, has not in the concrete accomplished liberation. It might be better to say, incidentally, not that Chesterton did not look at the problem of atheistic Communism from a religious point of view, but that he was answering a question that was both religious and social in a social way, precisely because the religious and the social constantly overlapped in his mind.

There is always a temptation for those who would right wrongs of this kind to advocate doing so in an authoritarian way, a temptation Chesterton never gave in to, despite the suspicions of some that he was sympathetic to Mussolini's Fascism. If he had any enthusiasm at all for Mussolini, it was at the very most short-lived, limited to the time when Chesterton did not see what Fascism implied. Although he clearly favored concerted action to right wrongs—and occasionally has a good word to say for a kind of "collectivism"—he clearly repudiates all forms of abstract classification of human beings, whether it be aristocratic talk of "the lower classes" or Marxist talk of "workers" who are not people who work but members of an abstract class.[32] This is not unrelated to his contention that, in righting wrongs, the primary thing to be done is not so much to identify the wrong and then right it as it is to identify the right and then rectify the wrong in light of the right. It is the whole definition and dignity of man, he contends, that in social matters we must actually find the cure before we find the disease. "I have called this book 'What's Wrong with the World' but the rather wild title refers only to one point. What is wrong is that we do not ask what is right."[33] Even revolution cannot be satisfied with merely knowing what is wrong; it demands firm belief that something is objectively right and permanent and should thus replace what is wrong: "For it stands to common sense that you cannot upset all existing things, customs, and compromises, unless you believe in something outside them, something positive and divine."[34] Precisely because Chesterton was so strongly committed to improving the world was he concerned to *know* what improvement was.

DISTRIBUTISM

Of one thing he was quite sure: that neither capitalism nor atheistic socialism was what the world needed, neither all property in the hands of an enormously wealthy minority nor all property abstractly owned by all but concretely controlled by government bureaucracy. As a mean between these two extremes—which he saw pretty much as two sides of the same coin—Chesterton consistently advocated the widest possible extension of private ownership of the means of production, convinced that in no other way would widespread poverty be effectively overcome and human dignity be convincingly maintained. Out of Chesterton's thinking and writing along these lines we can discern both a *theory* aimed at solving the socio-economic problems of the twentieth century and a *movement* geared to achieving the concrete implementation of the theory. The theory was that of "distributism," and the movement was the "Distributist League."

As was to be expected, Chesterton as a thinker was eminently qualified for thinking out the implications of the theory, but his organizing talents fell far short of the expertise necessary to make the movement concretely effective. There seems to be little need here, in a book dealing with Chesterton's thought and not to any extent with his biography, to treat what has already been handled admirably by biographers such as Maisie Ward, Margaret Canovan, and Alzina Stone Dale.[35] For our purposes here, what is important is not so much the practical success, or lack thereof, in putting into practice in other than isolated experiments distributist ideals. It is important, however, to say something about the thinking behind those ideals as presented in Chesterton's writings. Christopher Hollis[36] criticizes Chesterton not only from the practical point of view of organizational talent but also from the theoretical point of view of a failure to come to grips with the problem of an enormous increase in the world's population, which demands an extraordinarily elaborate system of industrial production simply to meet the needs of that population. To a degree, Hollis is correct, but by the same token it is also true that Hollis himself fails to show us that producing what is required to meet the needs of a vastly increased population must be accompanied by an obscene increase in the wealth and power of the wealthy or by a state structure that systematically ate away at the dignity and freedom of the poor. We have already seen that Chesterton had a very special love for and admiration of the poor, and it was this that prompted him to expend so much intellectual effort to make life more livable for them. It may very well be that in the present era of mass production and multi-national corporations there is no room for the practical implementation of the ideal of redistribution of property. It can certainly be said that distributist ideas have not found widespread acceptance in

today's world. By the same token, however, it can also be
said that the monopolistic mass production of multi-
national corporations would find no place in Chesterton's
moral universe, in which efficiency in material production
is not the ultimate measure of value, but the humanity
and personality of the individuals who make up society
are. It may very well be that Chesterton's view of the
Middle Ages was far too romantic to correspond with the
concrete reality of medieval society; he was still correct
in finding that the intellectual ideals of the Middle Ages
were more in accord with the dignity of the authentically
human than were the sweatshop attitudes of industrial
Britain. The enrichment of human life is far more significant than the expansion of a small number of bank ac-
counts. As Ronald Knox put it: "The body of ideas which
he labelled, rather carelessly, 'distributism' is a body of
ideas which still lasts, and I think will last, but it is not
exactly a doctrine, or a philosophy; it is simply Chesterton's reaction to life."[37] It is for this reason that we can
say, with Mario Amadeo, "The essence of Chesterton's
message has to be rescued, because it contains the only
effective proposals for humanising affluent societies and
recovering for them the spiritual patrimony they have
lost and almost forgotten."[38] It was not Chesterton's task
to draw up a blueprint for an effective distributist state—
although he did think of it as a concrete possibility—
rather it was by his thinking and writing to bring about
a revolution in values and ideas that could usher in a
more human way of living. One reason, it would seem,
that distributism has so far proved to be ineffectual is that
a major segment of the population, at least in the Western
world, has been conditioned by capitalism to take capitalism for granted. "Nowadays it is exactly those who have
here no abiding city who alone can build anything like a
city that will abide. It is exactly those who know that man

on earth is man in exile who can alone turn the earth into anything like a home."[39]

We cannot, of course, say that the modern trend toward a greater and greater loss of freedom has been reversed or even stemmed by Chesterton's intellectual efforts, but we can say that his writing constitutes an eloquent testimonial to the capacity of the human spirit to humanize itself. The pace of material development was, in Chesterton's age, insane, and the pace of human spiritual development was in inverse proportion to it. It is not without significance that he entitled a book, which grew out of a series of articles on this disproportion, *The Outline of Sanity*. As Maisie Ward says, "He was asking for a return to the sanity of field and workshop, of craftsman and peasant, from the insanity of trusts and machinery, of unemployment, over-production and starvation. 'We are destroying food because we do not need it. We are starving men because we do not need them.' "[40] It can, of course, seem unrealistic to look back to a form of economic society geared to satisfy the needs of a far smaller population to cure the ills of a far greater society of today. It might even be argued that the solution is not to get rid of machines—or even of trusts—but rather to humanize these (if that is conceivable). One thing is certain: the emphasis on making money, which is the contemporary goal of production, is a sure way of dehumanizing both production and life. Perhaps what is really needed is the capacity to see that what seems to be the most efficient mode of production is in the long run the least efficient because of the toll it takes in humanity.

One of the things, for example, that has turned science into a sacred cow is its capacity to provide the means to get even richer—without too much concern for the poor. In speaking of the very ideal of distributism, Lawrence

Clipper remarks that "alarm is generated by the endless aggrandizement of science,"[41] which is precisely what Chesterton saw happening. What is perhaps the greatest obstacle to improvement is still, as it was in Chesterton's day, the conviction on the part of those who might have the power and the resources to do something about it that the world is generally working quite well and would work even better if only the rest of the world would get on the capitalist bandwagon.

It might come as quite a surprise to some that Chesterton shared one very important conviction with Karl Marx, namely, that human beings distinguish themselves from the animals by working, which is to say by dominating matter in more and more ways. There are, it is true, significant differences in the positions of Marx and Chesterton. According to Marx, human beings distinguish themselves from the animals by working, in the sense that the work is transformative and lifts them above the animals, *thus* enabling them to think, to communicate, to cooperate. In Chesterton's view human beings are distinguished from animals *because* they are spiritual, not merely natural and, *therefore*, can work in such a way as to transform themselves into becoming more and more significantly spiritual. Another difference in their views is a corollary of this one. As we saw earlier, Chesterton could not see "workers" as designating a class to which certain humans belonged; rather "workmanship" is a quality that characterizes the human *qua* human, such that growth in being authentically human is a function of human work.

> What should be distributed is not merely the legal power of a man over money, but the divine or mystical power of a man over matter. Man is made man, after the fact that he prays, by the fact that he ploughs, that he builds, that he

cuts wood for transport or carves it for ornament; in short, by the fact that he has this mystical privilege of mastery over the material universe.[42]

This last points up another significant difference between Marx and Chesterton: for Marx this meant that all productive property should belong to *the* people, in the sense of the collectivity, such that the power could remain the prerogative of the *Party*; for Chesterton, productive property should belong to *people,* and it should be so widely distributed that monopoly—either of property or of power—could not take over. Finally, there is another significant similarity between the views of Marx and Chesterton: both see the very fact of "wages" turning human beings into commodities, whose work is bought by the owners of the means of production in order to make a profit—not for the ones who work but for the ones who own. One wonders sometimes why the super-patriots never got around to calling Chesterton a Marxist—or, more familiarly, a "Commie"—unless even they can see that distributism was just as opposed to communism as it was to capitalism. Chesterton may have been rather unrealistic about the practicality of remedying capitalism by substituting for it distributism; Marx, however, did make it clear that extremely large-scale private ownership of the means of production is *not* essential to efficient production.

One of the problems one must face in trying to write about distributism is that one is forced to refer to it in the past, not in either the present or the future. It might still be argued that it is desirable and even workable, but it cannot be argued that it was *desired* by enough people to make it work. The situation is not better now than it was in Chesterton's day; it is worse. Monopoly has not decreased; it has increased. It has become more difficult than ever for small ownership to survive, not even small farming; one wonders whether a peasantry is any longer even a possibility. Large-scale employers are becoming more and more large-scale—and more impersonal—and wage-earners are becoming increasingly enslaved. It may very well be that a much more equitable distribution of ownership is a social and even economic ideal, if freedom is to become a reality; but such an ideal needs political backing—needs politicians—if it is to be effectively implemented. Among the distributists one looks in vain for political savvy, and even Chesterton's rhetoric could do little to persuade those who did have political clout to do anything. In an essay entitled "A Misunderstanding about Method," Chesterton says, "I have finally decided to approach the social solution in this fashion: to point out first that the monopolist momentum is not irresistible; that even here and now much could be done to modify it, much by anybody, everything by everybody."[43] Unfortunately, however, he does not tell us to whom he is pointing this out, nor does he identify the "anybody" or "everybody" by whom so much could be done. He continues, "Then I would maintain that on the removal of that particular plutocratic pressure, the appetite and appreciation of natural property would revive, like any other natural thing."[44] One can, it is true, speak intelligibly—and intelligently—of "what would happen if," but that of itself does not get anything done, especially if the present system supplies "people" with more and cheaper goods. "Then, I say, it will be worthwhile to propound to people thus returning to sanity, however sporadically, a sane society that could balance property and control machinery."[45] It should be rather obvious that none of this will be practical without the enactment of laws that will make it possible, and once more the political becomes all important. Chesterton was aware of this last, but it is not clear that he really saw the difficulty of enacting the kind of laws he envisioned—without government coercion, which he deplored.

> Here . . . are half a dozen things which would help the process of Distributism, apart from those on which I shall have occasion to touch as point of principle. Not all Distributists would agree with all of them; but all would agree that they are in the direction of Distributism. (1) The taxation of contracts so as to discourage the sale of small property to big proprietors and encourage the break-up of big property among small proprietors. (2) Something like the Napoleonic testamentary law and the destruction of primogeniture. (3) The establishment of free law for the poor, so that small property could always be defended against great. (4) The deliberate protection of certain experiments in small property, if necessary by tariffs and even local tariffs. (5) Subsidies to foster the starting of such experiments. (6) A league of voluntary dedication, and any number of other things of the same kind.[46]

It certainly does not look as easy as he would like to have it seem. If what we have, as Chesterton says, is a plutocracy, where political power and wealth go hand in hand, it is not easy to see how reform will be possible without enlisting the support of the rich, and the formula for that is scarcely forthcoming. It should not be difficult to recognize the revolutionary character of distributism, but neither should it be difficult to comprehend that revolution cannot be confined to the dissemination of ideas, no matter how heady they may be. There is, however, one very practical truth made available to us in this war of ideas: nothing at all will happen, no improvement in the social situation will be forthcoming, if responsible human beings do not freely act in such a way as to bring about change, and where there are no guiding ideas there is no free, responsible action. This, incidentally, hits right at the nerve-center of Distributism as a movement: all too frequently the action it called for was not well thought out—even though its principles were well thought out—with the result that the action accomplished little and did little to establish the desirability of Distributism as a solution to real evils. Add to this that Distributism demands the kind of sacrifice that few people are willing to make, and the likelihood of its success is diminished even more.

> In my opinion the Distributist League was before its times. In our day and generation no socio-economic political program demands such a change of heart among masses of ordinary people as does distributism. . . . A popular change of heart is notoriously a long process (short of widespread catastrophe); and if it be in the direction of unselfish, simplified and not-easy ways of life, how much longer?[47]

In any event, it is simply a fact that the distributist movement did not succeed, and an important reason for that was, in the words of Maisie Ward, "the proneness of certain Distributists to act first and think later."[48] Being in a hurry is not a contribution to a movement such as this.

CHESTERTON'S "MEDIEVALISM"

Chesterton has more than once been taken to task for his rather romantic attachment to the Middle Ages and, particularly, for his admiration for medieval peasantry, which serves him as a kind of model for the virtues of small ownership. It is true, of course, that he did idealize medieval culture to such an extent that he failed to take adequate account of the social, political, and economic inequities that plagued that culture. It is not true, however, that he advocated a return to medievalism. To do justice to his attachment to the Middle Ages, we must first come to grips with the blindness that existed in his day, particularly in Britain, to the virtues of medieval culture. It was as though history had taken a grand leap from Ancient to Renaissance culture, leaving in between nothing but the "barbarism" of the "Dark Ages." John Ruskin, it is true, had done much to rescue the art and architecture of the Middle Ages, but he completely failed to appreciate medieval philosophy and theology, nor did he recognize that the Renaissance itself was the product of an educational process which was kept alive in the "schools" of the Middle Ages. If, then, Chesterton was loud in his praises of the Middle Ages, particularly of medieval saints like Francis of Assisi and Thomas Aquinas, of medieval poets like Chaucer and Dante, of the medieval art of the Romanesque and the Gothic, it was primarily to combat the obscurantism that saw the Middle Ages only in terms of ignorance. That such obscurantism is no longer popular is due in large measure to those who, like Chesterton, never ceased to proclaim the spiritual heritage—artistic, intellectual, religious—bequeathed to us by the Middle Ages.

What Chesterton was *not* trying to do, however, was to ask for a return to medieval social order; we can drink deep of the medieval spirit without that kind of return. One can be a *laudator temporis acti* without canonizing all that pertains to that *tempus actum*. By the same token, a whole era cannot be characterized by what pertains only to its best minds. It is nevertheless true, and Chesterton was right to emphasize it, that a more equitable distribution of property could go a long way toward renewing a vital spirit without restoring an outmoded social structure. What Chesterton seems not to have realized, however, was that the distributist revolution he envisaged could not be accomplished short of a political revolution, which would inevitably run the risk of generating totalitarianism, as it did in Germany, Russia, Italy, Spain, and Portugal, and as it has to a very great extent done in Central and Eastern Europe. In theory, Distributism aims at the restoration of liberty, and it may very well be that, if there were enough good will going around, it could succeed in just that, but one has to wonder if what it sought to overcome had become an ingrained tendency in human nature, which only a despotic revolution could overcome. We have already seen the kind of legislation Chesterton advocated to enable Distributism to take hold, but one has to ask what kind of government could be persuaded to enact such legislation. One does not have to deny that distributism is a pre-eminently worthwhile ideal in order to see the perhaps insuperable difficulty of realizing it among human beings pre-conditioned to the acceptance of its antithesis. It may well be that anything is preferable to "Big Business" or "Big Brother," but how to galvanize a whole society into effective action?

Here it is that it becomes necessary to dredge up regarding Chesterton something which has been misunderstood both by those who attack him and by those who defend him. It is the question of Chesterton's alleged anti-Semitism. What this has to do with the distributist ideal may not be immediately evident, but the language he used, which to a great extent is responsible for the charge against him, was a language forged in the ongoing battle with great wealth, which battle engaged him throughout his adult life. It is a violent language; to a great extent it is a tendentious language; it is clearly an unfortunate language, as the language of controversy tends to be, but it was *not* an anti-Semitic language. One of the difficulties I constantly encounter in this dispute is that I look in vain among the disputants for a precise notion of what anti-Semitism means. As I see it, anti-Semitism here means either opposition to or hatred of the Jewish people (looked upon as a "race") or ethnic group as such. Chesterton did *not* hate any race or ethnic group, even though he had many unkind things to say about Americans, or Prussians, or Scotsmen, or Japanese, or Jews—race was not the reason; how he experienced people as people was the reason. In *Heretics* he says very pointedly: "Of all forms in which science or pseudo-science has come to the rescue of the rich and the stupid, there is none so singular as the singular invention of the theory of *races*."[49] This is not the "some-of-his-best-friends-were-Jews" type of argument; it is a recognition that he frequently said "Jew" when he meant "wealthy Jewish monopolist"—which is unfortunate but not anti-Semitic, even though today we can see no reason for the emphasis on "Jewish." We must also realize that forms of expression, which today we rightly call intolerable, were not experienced as intolerable by readers in the first three decades of this century, none of which means that we should simply ignore the to us intolerable language.

When all is said and done, there is an unforgivable arbitrariness—which we who have grown up in New York City, for example, have experienced since childhood—in employing ethnic terms as abusive, terms such as "Kraut," "Spic," "Dago," "Nigger," "Mick." Even more unforgivable, however, is the employment of a perfectly legitimate term like "Jew" abusively—even if one does not intend it to be all-inclusively abusive, frequently there is no good reason to employ the term at all. What is, perhaps, most unforgivable in Chesterton's attitude to Jews was his conviction that they could never be full-scale Englishmen—or Frenchmen, or Americans—because their primary loyalty was to their own people, their own "nation." Even in his advocacy of Zionism one has to detect more interest in getting the Jews *out* of England than in getting them *into* a land of their own. It is, however, rather remarkable that in his own day there was no hue and cry, whether from Jews or others, over the language he used. He was violent in his condemnation of the venal behavior of the Isaacs brothers, Rufus and Godfrey, in the Marconi scandal, yet no one seemed to think that he

was picking on them because they were Jewish; if anything, his behavior was applauded because it manifested
courage in the face of power. It does not cease to be unfortunate that he so frequently identified those whose
values he opposed as "Jews," but it may well be that we
are far more sensitive to that than were his contemporaries. When Ian Boyd, for example, speaks of the crude
and almost schoolboy quality of much of Chesterton's
anti-Semitism,[50] he may well be saying something true,
but it should be noted that he is saying it in 1975. It is
not without significance, too, that *G. K.'s Weekly*,
which began publication in 1925 and continued for eleven
years, does not contain any remarks that can in any way
be reasonably interpreted as anti-Semitic. What I find far
more amazing than his alleged anti-Semitism, which is
aimed at the wealthy and the powerful, is his complete
lack of sympathy with blacks, whom he consistently refers to as "niggers" (always scornfully), or sometimes as
"wooly savages." There seems little doubt that, like most
Englishmen, he quite clearly looked upon blacks as inferior to whites (he extends the unfortunate comparison
to Asiatics too). During the Boer War in South Africa, he
made himself quite unpopular in England by favoring
the cause of the Boers against the British, but he seems
to have given no consideration to the cause of the native
Africans in relation to either the British or the Boers.
There seems little doubt that he considered being a black
—or even being married to one—a misfortune.[51] Nor
does it serve any purpose to say that he thought as did any
Englishman in his day; one looks for something better in
Chesterton! One simply finds it difficult to reconcile a
statement such as "He who believes in the existence of
God believes in the equality of men"[52] with what seems
to be a conviction that blacks are *not* equal.

When it comes to Chesterton's attitude toward women,

more subtlety is required in determining just what that attitude was. There are two constants in his thought on the subject: (1) men and women are absolutely equal; and (2) men and women are very different. There is no reason to gainsay either of these contentions, but it turns out to be a question of emphasis. When it comes to the procreation of children—perhaps even to the nurture of children—the difference certainly makes a difference, but it is not certain that Chesterton's insistence on difference does not overstate the case. He was clearly anti-feminist in his views, but we must remember that the feminism in question was that of the "suffragettes" of the first two decades of this century. That he was against giving the franchise to women I simply do not understand, but he was certainly not in the minority—where, presumably, he belonged—in Britain. Perhaps the best we can say is that Chesterton throughout his life remained quite Victorian in many of his views. There can be little doubt that he thought he was doing women a favor by trying to prevent their becoming too much like men, but even in this one detects a certain condescendence. He saw men and women as by nature equipped to occupy two distinct spheres of activity and influence in relation to the preservation of the human family: for men, the world of politics and business; for women, the world of the home and the training of children; for both, creative roles in making the world a better place to live in—men through cleverness, women through wisdom. For Chesterton there was always the question of the proper balance; for men and women equality, yes, sameness, no. Whether he himself always maintained that delicate balance may well be a moot question; his attitudes, however, were not irrational, even when they were inadequate. Above all, he was not irrational in his opposition to a prevalent blind faith in the dogma of progress, which looked upon change as inevitably improvement and upon a return to the past as inevitably retrogression. There must always remain open the possibility of a return to the past, if we are to be able to find ourselves.[53] In one sense Chesterton always had both his feet firmly planted on the ground; in another, his feet were always dancing in midair, because he was essentially a mystic, one who consistently maintained the delicate balance between rational truth and mystery.

> To explain this peculiar kind of public value one must understand one of the deepest differences, and perhaps diseases, of our time. It was the mark of the art of the past, especially the art of the Renaissance, that the great man was a man. He was an extraordinary man, but only in the sense of being an ordinary man with something extra. Shakespeare or Rubens went with the plain man as far as the plain man went; they ate and drank, and desired and died as he did. That is what people mean when they say that these gods had feet of clay; their giant boots were heavy with the mire of the earth. That is what people mean when they say that Shakespeare was often coarse; that is what people mean when they say that he was often dull. They mean that a great poet of the elder kind had spaces which were idle and absent-minded; that his sub-consciousness often guided him; that he sprawled; that he was not "artistic." It is not only true that Homer sometimes nodded; but nodding was part of the very greatness of Homer. His sleepy nod shakes the stars like the nod of his own Jupiter.[54]

He liked to think of himself as the "ordinary man," which he most certainly was not—unless, of course, we can see "ordinary" as proximately derived from "order."

> The ordinary man has always been sane because the ordinary man has always been a mystic. . . . He has always cared more for truth than for consistency. If he saw two truths that seemed to contradict each other, he would take the two truths and the contradiction along with them. His spiritual sight is stereoscopic, like his physical sight: he sees two different pictures at once and yet sees all the better for that.

Thus he has always believed that there was such a thing as fate, but such a thing as free will also. Thus he believed that children were indeed the kingdom of heaven, but nevertheless ought to be obedient to the kingdom of earth. He admired youth because it was young and age because it was not. It is exactly this balance of apparent contradictions that has been the whole buoyancy of the healthy man.[55]

It is of particular interest that Chesterton himself should have linked this to the Aristotelian concept of the "mean" between extremes, when it comes to "virtue"—and here we could speak of the virtue of "sanity."[56] The working out of this sanity of balance we shall see in what can be called Chesterton's "humanism," which is human because it is Christian, and Christian because it is so quintessentially human.

6

Chesterton's Christian Humanism

FROM ALL THAT WE HAVE SEEN up to this point it would seem that we shall ultimately appreciate Chesterton only if we see in him one who was inebriated with the marvel of reality, with existence, with life, with being human. It is in this sense that we can appropriately say that he was a "humanist," if by that we mean one who at once appreciated the grandeur of the human and made every effort both to grow more authentically human and to help others to grow in the same way. It is important to note, however, that what he considered to be the grandeur of the human did not consist in being distinguished by talent, success, reputation, or power, but rather to be distinguished by an acute awareness of being the recipient of a tremendous gift to which the only adequate response is everlasting gratitude. It is precisely for this that Chesterton has to be called a "Christian humanist," because he was so keenly aware that humanism is not to be equated with the elitism of the Renaissance, the rationalism of the Enlightenment, or the naturalism of the Victorian Age. Still less is it to be equated with the "Promethean" humanism of those who find God to be a threat to human dignity.

In our own age, to be sure, one does hesitate to employ the term "humanist" in an honorific sense, precisely because the label has been monopolized by those who, like Marx, Nietzsche, Freud, or Sartre, have set up an artificial and unjustified axiological rivalry between the human and the divine—the supposition being that to up-

grade the one is to downgrade the other—and then have
opted for the human over the divine, thus engaging in
what is called a "Promethean" rebellion. The intention
of all this is to enhance the glory of the human by dis-
pensing entirely with the divine, failing to realize that all
that has been accomplished is the creation of a tender and
unneeded protectionism of the human, a wanting to be
tough-minded that succeeds only in being tender-hearted.
What this attitude fails to see, and what Chesterton toiled
so tirelessly to elucidate, is that the relationship to God
is an essential dimension of the human, constitutive of
the human, without which the human is not authentically
human. What we have to realize, as Chesterton sees it, is
that to insist on the inseparability of humanistic and religious values, of the human and the divine—which is to
say, of the dependence of the human on the divine—in
no way impugns the dignity of the human at all; it still
recognizes that the task of human development is a task
of human self-development, of human initiative, wherein
the human being is seen as an integrated whole, a dy-
namic whole, a wholeness of action integrated in the agent
who is a person, not a mere machine or even a mere organism. Chestertonian humanism, then, is a direct de-
scendent of medieval humanism, predicated on a unity of
faith; it explains Chesterton's emphasis on medieval culture and his desire to serve that unified faith, with a
profound sense of his responsibility as an individual to
society, which sense of responsibility he considered to be
a deeply ingrained characteristic of the medieval artist—
and thinker. All that needs to be added is that Chesterton
meant all this quite literally, even though, as we saw in
the preceding chapter, his own appreciation of black and
Asiatic human beings was less than spectacular.

It is by no means without significance that, in Chesterton's day, the Middle Ages were commonly called the

"Dark Ages," that period in history when, again presumably, faith rather than rational inquiry guided human destinies—as though faith and rational inquiry were mutually exclusive. Chesterton is not saying that the Middle Ages were suffused with the clear light of rational thought; he *is* saying that medieval thinkers were more rational—even more logical—than his own disdainful contemporaries, and that the Christian heritage of the Middle Ages exudes a clarity of thought that has largely been lost in a secularized world. It was this that enabled him to say of Chaucer, "The great poet exists to show the small man how great he is";[1] "The great poet is alone strong enough to measure that broken strength we call the weakness of man."[2] It must be doubted, after all, that an authentic humanist could ever look on other human beings as "inferior." One thing that Chesterton never was was an elitist; he saw humanity "not as an abstraction but as the sum of human and intensely individual beings."[3]

> The mountain tops are only noble because from them we are privileged to behold the plains. So the only value in any man being superior is that he may have superior admiration for the level and the common. If there is any profit in a place craggy and precipitous it is only because from the vale it is not easy to see all the beauty of the vale; because when actually in the flats one cannot see their sublime and satisfying flatness. If there is any value in being educated and eminent (which is doubtful enough) it is only because the best instructed man may feel most swiftly and certainly the splendour of the ignorant and the simple: the full magnificence of that mighty human army in the plains.[4]

When we understand this about Chesterton, then we can also understand just what his love of truth was: not the desire for an abstract grasp of what can be affirmed or denied, but rather the orientation of the mind to precisely that truth without which it cannot be true to itself. In this light, then, humanism is not a doctrine or a theory;

it is a task, the task of becoming all that it is to be truly human, of realizing in our lives what each one of us is, the *imago Dei*, which makes sense only as the self-creative image of the Creator God. If this means anything, it means the self-development of all that is best in human potentialities. But that too poses a problem: What is the criterion for a development that is good rather than bad; granted that to be human is to be rich in potentialities, what potentialities are best—or even just plain good? The line between what is strength and what is weakness in the human is indeed thin, and to discern which is which is a question of wisdom, of distinguishing between that which makes for wholeness and that which makes for fragmentation. Here it is that one of Chesterton's most famous aphorisms may find its place. "The Christian ideal," he says, "has not been tried and found wanting. It has been found difficult; and left untried."[5] To which we might add that the Christian ideal will always be at odds with the trivial "evolutionist" contention that, if there is development, it is *eo ipso* good.

It should be noted at this point that the term "humanism" is thoroughly neutral. Of itself it bespeaks little more than a vague conviction that human life on this earth is supremely important, that the aim of life is the cultivation of all that is best in human potentialities, that the enhancement of human living is the supreme goal of human activity—a human endeavor to promote the human—all of which are quite capable of being little more than elegant words with no identifiable substance behind them. These convictions, of course, may very well be valid (even though they consistently tend to exclude the greater portion of the human race from the realization of the ideal), but they are meaningful only against the backdrop of the image of man on which they are predicated. Only where its image of man is authentic does the concept of "humanism" make sense at all; the most assiduous cultivation of the inauthentically human is inhuman, and frequently the line between what is strength and what is weakness in the human is amazingly thin. There is a very real sense in which all "isms" are humanisms, because each is an ideological platform from which its adherents can launch their views as to what is the best way to be human, each thoroughly confident in the adequacy of its answer.[6]

There can be no question, of course, that a humanism that emphasizes the essential dignity of being human is putting emphasis where emphasis needs to be put, provided it is accompanied by a clear idea of just what "human" is to mean—or, perhaps, come to mean. We *need* to be reminded that there is no substitute for personal responsibility in human affairs, especially at a time when shirking that responsibility is becoming endemic to a generation that needs but to roll up the windows of its cars or sit in closed rooms before its private television screens to shut out from consciousness the life that seethes around it. We need to be reminded that human integrity is inseparable from the integrality of the human person, that trust in human nature must displace mistrust if we are not all to be misanthropes, or cynics—following Chesterton's definition of the cynic as "the man who knows the price of everything but the value of nothing."[7] It is simply fatuous to ignore an essential dimension of the human, without which no one is integrally human. The relationship to God is specifically human, such that a failure to acknowledge that relationship can result only in a truncated view of what it means to be human.

THEOLOGY OF THE HUMAN

The late nineteenth and early twentieth centuries developed such an adoration of nature—and particularly of the so-called "laws" of nature—that they looked to nature to explain everything and thus to do away with all mystery. In so doing, not only did they not abolish mystery, but they rendered the most mysterious of all mysteries, i.e., man, more mysterious than ever. There can be no question that the present century has seen more dramatic and extensive advances in the sciences of nature than have the millennia that preceded it. There can be no question either, however, that the result of trying to understand the human spirit as no more than a product of nature has been an enormous falsification of that spirit. The focus of all Chesterton's enormous output—literary criticism, poetry, biographies, novels, detective stories, the endless stream of essays, social, political, moral, religious—had but one ultimate end in view: to bring human beings to an ever-greater realization of the marvel of being human, a realization that was blocked in his day by the "heresy" of seeing human beings as simply the product of nature. He had to make it clear: (1) that nothing is a product of nature, since nature is not a producer but only a mode of production; and (2) that the human individual is unique *in* nature as the only such being that images, not merely points to, God, and this the human being does by being creative: "Art is the signature of man."[8] Nature alone, be it inanimate or animate, does not produce works of art; yet it can be said that it is natural for human beings to produce what nature of itself cannot produce.[9]

It is not enough, however, that human beings can produce what nature cannot produce; there is a very real sense in which it is the task of humans to bring the human into being. By being creative the human becomes more human, thus imaging God more and more. "It seems to me nearer to the true Christian tradition to hold that man creates in his capacity of the image of God; and he is in nothing so much the image of God as in creating images."[10] To which we might add that the human, creative image of God is God's own self-manifestation, both *in* the human and *to* the human. All talk of this kind, however, runs the risk of turning into a kind of humanist jumble without the theological doctrine of the Incarnation, according to which God (*a*) glorifies the human by divinizing it in Jesus Christ, and (*b*) selects out of the infinite potentialities of the human those which will make the human person most resemble the divine Person who became man, the second Person of the Trinity.[11] In a manner reminiscent of Hegel, who assuredly did not influence him on this point, Chesterton speaks of the Incarnation as the divine revelation of the unique importance of the human—not only in general but as individual.

> There is in that alone the touch of a revolution, as of the world turned upside down. It would be vain to attempt to say anything adequate, or anything new, about the change which this conception of a deity born like an outcast or even an outlaw had upon the whole conception of law and its duties to the poor and outcast. It is profoundly true to say that after that moment there could be no slaves. There could be no more of the pagan repose in the mere advantage to the state of keeping it a servile state. Individuals became important, in a sense in which no instruments can be important. A man could not be a means to an end, at any rate to any other man's end.[12]

(One has to wonder whether Chesterton perhaps knew the philosophers better than we think he did; the last sentence, after all, is reminiscent of Kant.)

In any event he was making no effort to soften the literal affirmation of the divinity of Christ, without which Christianity is not even a religion.

> These saints [St. Francis and St. Thomas] were, in the most exact sense of the term, Humanists; because they were insisting on the immense importance of the human being in the theological scheme of things. . . . They were strengthening that staggering doctrine of Incarnation, which the sceptics find it hardest to believe. There cannot be a stiffer piece of Christian divinity than the divinity of Christ.[13]

To which we might add that nothing can enable us better to appreciate the marvel of the human than the unity of the divine and the human in Christ, the Image of God who is himself God. Considering the unfathomable differences of human beings from each other, it is difficult to recognize equality of all as real, except insofar as all are equal in imaging God and insofar as Christ the Son of God is the model of all imaging. Taking this revealed truth, which reason can only applaud, not discover, then it is possible to see philosophically, as Chesterton does, following Thomas Aquinas, that reason is that within us which "has a right to rule, as the representative of God in man."[14] The reason which dwells *in* us is God's revelation of himself *to* us. It is this self-revelation of God in us and to us that makes democratic equality not only possible but necessary. Margaret Canovan has aptly caught the unity of Christian belief and political wisdom in Chesterton's vision of the defiled human image of God: "It seemed to Chesterton that Christianity, besides providing the strict rule that the rebel needs if he is to be effective, also provided the only sound basis for democracy; the twin beliefs that all men are made in the image of God (even the poor) and that all men are tainted with Original Sin (even the rich)."[15] There is unfortunately a tendency in modern times to put so much emphasis on the imperfections of the human as to cloud the divine image which the human is. It is all very well to point out that it is human to make mistakes; it is just as important to point out that it is also quite human to correct mistakes. "The specially and outstandingly human things are exactly the things that you dismiss as merely divine things. The human things are free will and responsibility and authority and self-denial, because they exist only in humanity";[16] which is but another way of saying that among beings in nature only human beings image divine Being.

It has been remarked by more than a few commentators that Chesterton, even after his conversion to the Catholic Church, has relatively little to say about the Eucharist, either as sacrament or as sacrifice. Why this is, we really do not know, but a remark he makes in *Sidelights* (1932) indicates his profound awareness of the link between the divine revelation of the human in the Incarnation and the same revelation in the Eucharist: "But the Mass is exactly the opposite of a Man seeking to be a God. It is a God seeking to be a Man; it is God giving his creative life to mankind as such, and restoring the original pattern of their manhood; making not gods, nor beasts, nor angels; but, by the original blast and miracle that makes all things new, turning men into men."[17] In all of this incarnational language, of course, there is hidden a profound warning against so spiritualizing the human as to forget that the human is truly human only as the unity of spirit *and* matter: "A man is not a man without his body, just as he is not a man without his soul."[18] To insist thus on the integrality of the human union of spirit and matter, on the other hand, is to insist on the freedom and the responsibility of the human *qua* spiritual being. "Upon this sublime and perilous liberty hang heaven and hell, and all the mysterious drama of the soul. It is distinction and not division, but a man *can* divide himself from God, which, in a certain aspect, is the greatest distinction of all."[19] What all this spells out, then, is the glory of the human, as a gift from God; to be created human by God is to be specially "gifted," in the original sense of having received gifts![20]

It is not easy for us today to recognize the courage exhibited by Chesterton in at once championing the glory of being human and combating with all his energy the merely pagan humanism that held the field in his day. From 1900 to 1922 he fought the battle against paganism as a Christian committed to the defense of the divine message for human beings contained in the Good News of Jesus Christ. From 1922 on, he drew the battle lines more sharply by opting to follow the teaching of the Roman Catholic Church, which, to many of his contemporaries, made him seem at the very least to be most un-English and, therefore, not to be listened to. That it made him at the same time the darling of the indiscriminate adulation of an embattled Catholic minority, many of whom were more concerned with being instructed as to what to think than with being challenged to think for themselves, must also be taken into consideration. There were many who asked why it took Chesterton so long to become a Roman Catholic, since it is fairly obvious that all along he sympathized with that sort of thinking. There were others who felt that, in making that move, he was losing ground, which latter answer may give in some degree an answer to the first question.

As I see it, conversion to Catholicism was not just a question of what teaching satisfied him most as an individual; far more was it a question of deciding where he could do the most good in the battle against modern paganism. It was not the first time, nor will it be the last, that the question is placed very concretely before the consciousness—and the conscience—of the serious militant. Alzina Stone Dale has put the matter quite succinctly, saying:

> By joining the Roman Catholic Church, however worldwide its body, Chesterton was becoming the proud, naturalized citizen of an endangered small nation, a nation not highly thought of in England. In this way, Chesterton was also reaffirming his sense of identity with the "secret people." He amiably put up with the fact that the Roman Catholic Church made use of him, taking comfort from also being a part of a special, worldwide family.[21]

One of the things that attracted Chesterton to the Roman Catholic Church—an experience common to many converts in the twentieth century—was that it had clearly defined positions, religious, moral, social, which one could not only clearly identify but also identify *with*; those who, he claimed, preferred to identify with broad, universal ideas rather than with narrow, sectarian ideas were, more often than not, caught in the very narrowness of their "broad" ideas. Atheists are narrow-minded, agnostics are narrow-minded, bigots are narrow-minded, precisely because they cannot stretch their minds to the richness of experience. The largeness of experience is what he claims to have found in the demands Catholicism made on him: "The largeness of the other schemes is an unreal largeness of generalization, whereas the largeness of our scheme is a real largeness of experience."[22] It is also a largeness that comes from not confining its love of the human to the merely human but from recognizing that the authenticity of the human is inseparable from the divinity of the human.[23] It is precisely for this reason that Christian thought can accord such great dignity to the human, because the human it can admire is never merely human. The secular humanists who love all human beings simply because of their dignity and lovableness are bound to find out sooner or later that, if all there is to love in the human is what is natural, the human is not so lovable after all.[24] To discover, however, that a humanism that focuses only on the human is not adequate as an attitude is to begin to come to the realization that the world of modern humanism is living on values bequeathed to it by an ancient Christian tradition.

That fact is this: the modern world, with its modern movements, is living on its Catholic capital. It is using, and using up, the truths that remain to it out of the old treasury of Christendom; including, of course, many truths known to pagan antiquity but crystallized in Christendom. But it is *not* really starting new enthusiasms of its own. The novelty is a matter of names and labels, like modern advertisement; in almost every other way the novelty is merely negative. It is not starting fresh things that it can really carry on far into the future. On the contrary, it is picking up old things that it cannot carry on at all.[25]

Various attempts have been made to de-sacralize the inherited values, but the result of that is at best devaluation, not revaluation—above all not "transvaluation."[26]

THE HUMAN NEED OF RELIGION

Although the fame of G. K. Chesterton is celebrated for the most part primarily by Roman Catholics, who find in him an extraordinary apologete for their faith, it has to be pointed out that, as early as 1901 (21 years before his conversion to Catholicism), he was already making known to his readers his conviction of the indispensability of religion, if life was to be lived to its fullest. Against the arguments current around the turn of the century that all religion has its source in superstition, he argued that religion would survive as long as the human race survives, because it is pre-eminently human to need religion.

> For the truth is that there will always be religions so long as certain primeval facts of life remain inexplicable and therefore religious. Such things as birth and death and dreams are at once so impenetrable and so provocative that to ask men to put them on one side, and have no hopes or theories about them, is like asking them not to look at a comet or not to look out the answer of a riddle. . . . But if we take a large and lucid view of the main history of mankind we shall be driven to the conclusion that nothing is upon the whole so natural as supernaturalism.[27]

It could, of course, be argued that, just because it is natural for humans to be religious, it is not necessary that to be religious is to be true. Nor is Chesterton saying this; what he is saying is that to be religious is to be healthy, and to be irreligious is to be unhealthy. It is important to realize that it is natural for human beings to be more than merely natural. He could not tolerate an indefensible dualism of body and spirit, but neither could he tolerate the naïve refusal to recognize a distinction between the spiritual and the material. "Religion is only the responsible reinforcement of common courage and common sense. Religion only sets up the normal mood of health against the hundred moods of disease."[28] Again, one might counter that to say this is to prove nothing. To which the rather obvious retort is that Chesterton was not trying to "prove" anything, he was trying to help people *see* differently—or to show those who already saw the way he himself did that seeing the way they did was quite healthy. To have done this, however, is to have shown that true religion is at the heart of happiness, not of unhappiness, and the whole of *Orthodoxy* (1908) is geared to making this clear: "And it did cross my mind that, perhaps, those might not be the very best judges of the relation of religion to happiness who, by their own account, had neither one nor the other."[29] There is no need to deny that there can be sick religiosity in order to affirm that authentic religious conviction is healthy.

There should be no reason to dispute that religion, in the many forms it has taken down through the centuries, has always been an eloquent expression of a profound need of the human heart, whether that heart be primitive, civilized, or cultivated. That need has expressed itself in the manifold mythological and poetic expressions of paganism, a wistful reaching out to a divinity which constantly recedes in paganism, ancient and modern. It expressed itself—and still does—in the heroic clinging of the Jewish people to the one God who revealed himself to the people he had chosen to be his own, a people whose history has been one of repeated and ghastly suffering, but never a history of tragedy, because tragedy can be only where there is no hope, and hope has never ceased to characterize that people. It has expressed itself in Christianity as a profound need not only of the human heart but also of the human head. Chesterton could never be satisfied with a religion that spoke to his emotions but not to his intellect. It may seem strange to some of us that it took twenty-two years for him to answer the call that was going out to him from the religion of Rome, but it should not seem strange to any of us that precisely high intellectuality can make hearing the call a slow process. One thing is abundantly clear: Chesterton's lifelong quest for truth was primarily an intellectual quest—even though not without its affective overtones—which repeatedly revealed to him that what his reason told him to be true turned out to be what the Church had been teaching all along. "He began as an agnostic, found that agnosticism did not satisfy his intellect, set himself to find out what *would* satisfy his intellect, and when he found it, was astonished to see that his own brand-new notions were the same as the ancient doctrines of the Church."[30] What we might say is this: as early as 1906 when he wrote *Heretics*—and certainly by the time he wrote *Orthodoxy* in 1908—Chesterton had come to the realization that Christianity was unique among religions in combining reason and faith. It then took many more years for the realization to break through that the intimate union of reason and faith antedated the Reformation and was proper to the old, undivided Church. "The truth is that the Church was actually the first thing that ever tried to combine reason and religion. There had never before been any such union of the priests and the philosophers."[31] In a unique way, the Church, as he saw it, spoke at once to head and heart:

> It [the Church] met the mythological search for romance by being a story and the philosophical search for truth by being a true story. That is why the ideal figure had to be a historical character, as nobody had ever felt Adonis or Pan to be a historical character. But that is also why the historical character had to be the ideal figure; and even fulfill many of the functions given to these other ideal figures; why he was at once the sacrifice and the feast, why he could be shown under the emblems of the growing vine or the rising sun. The more deeply we think of the matter the more we shall conclude that, if there be indeed a God, his creation could hardly have reached any other culmination than this granting of a real romance to the world.[32]

It is not without significance in this connection that Christian art is richly theological, thus speaking to both head and heart in telling its theological story.[33] It was this story that he saw spelled out all over the face of Britain as its medieval heritage. Admittedly, nothing of what has been said here demands that we agree with everything Chesterton's head or heart (or both) told him, but neither need we assert our independence to the extent of denying that he makes a good rational case for his religious convictions. In an age in which concepts such as "religion" and "faith" have become so vague that it is frequently difficult to determine whether they have any content whatever, it is refreshing to re-read Chesterton and to find that the two concepts have very definite and definitive meanings for him. They are by no means synonymous, but neither are they separable. Both imply not only acceptance of but also commitment to truth whose source is not merely rational thinking; both are supernatural and are, hence, not rationally explicable; and yet, if they are not susceptible of rational investigation and formulation, they are empty—to believe and not to know what it is one believes is not to believe in any meaningful sense of the term. Faith can be seen either as the subjective activity of believing or as the objective sum-total of what is believed. Religion, on the other hand, consists in what one *does* about what one believes. If, for example, I believe that because all human beings are, as children of God, equal, I cannot stop at that abstract affirmation; I must *treat* them as equals. By the same token, if I believe that God is a Trinity of persons, I cannot ignore the role of the relation of persons to persons as constitutive of personhood; if I believe that one person of this Trinity became authentically human, I cannot ignore the lesson this tells me about being authentically human—the inescapable union of freedom and responsibility.

Chesterton, however, goes further than this—at least after his conversion to the Roman Catholic Church. Faith, for him, meant acceptance of and commitment to a *body* of revealed truths, defined as such by competent authority, which body of revealed truths is what we call a creed. It also means that much of one's manner of behaving is called forth by the creed one affirms. What was difficult for many in Chesterton's day to accept, particularly the "intellectuals," who were convinced that only "science" had infallible answers, was the conviction that what one affirmed, even though it was not known scientifically, was nevertheless true and its opposite not true. This continues to be a difficulty in a world where faith is equated with ungrounded subjective conviction, and religion is taken to be a private emotional affair. What was even more offensive to his contemporaries, however, and continues to be so, was Chesterton's contention that he found the creed as a body of beliefs acceptable, because it corresponded to his experience of the realities of life, because he found that its acceptance liberated rather than imprisoned him, gave him a way of life he could live with.

> We accept it [the creed]; and the ground is solid under our feet and the road is open before us. It does not imprison us in a dream of destiny or a consciousness of the universal delusion. It opens to us not only incredible heavens, but what seems to some an equally incredible earth, and makes it credible. This is the sort of truth that is hard to explain because it is a fact; but it is a fact to which we can call witnesses. We are Christians and Catholics not because we worship a key, but because we have passed a door; and felt the wind that is the trumpet of liberty blow over the land of the living.[34]

It is for this reason that he could contend, more and more forcefully and confidently as time went on, that what he affirmed by way of belief he did with both conviction and enthusiasm.[35] In addition, he was also convinced that the Christian religion was the only religion that had a creed in the strict sense of the term,[36] and that the creed was indeed a creed because it was the official teaching of the ancient, undivided church of Jesus Christ.[37] It was in this Church in his own day that he found the representative of sanity and common sense, and to do that, he was convinced, was to find dogma, as that which had to be believed, because it was taught authoritatively by the only authority that could do so.

None of this, of course, demands that we accept as authoritative *teaching* all that Chesterton claims to be so. If there was one fundamental belief that undergirded all else that Chesterton believed in his later years it was the belief that the Catholic Church still speaks with the voice of Jesus Christ. There is, to be sure, a tendency in Chesterton—as there is in so many converts, particularly English converts—to ignore what John Henry Newman called "the development of dogma," such that Chesterton will look upon as definitive for all future time positions which at least *can* be modified with the passage of time. There is, for example, the possibility that the last word has not been said on intransigent positions that have been presented as the Church's definitive teaching. It is conceivable at least that certain rigid positions could become more nuanced, as we have already seen: e.g., the categorical prohibition of so-called "artificial" birth control, the unqualified insistence on the indissolubility of marriage, the refusal even to discuss the ordination of women or the necessity of clerical celibacy, the meaningfulness of inherited sin, the precise meaning and function of "infallibility," etc., etc. The Church has always recognized an important distinction between dogma and discipline, and the distinction should not be blurred. In *Heretics*, Chesterton had recommended that the world go on a long journey and "seek until we have discovered our own opinions."[38] There is no reason why conversion should be the end of all seeking, or that, in the light of faith, all "opinions" should become dogmas. On the other hand, faith is more than an affirmation that certain propositions are true; it is an affirmation that the truth believed in makes a difference as to the way life is lived. It is in this sense that fine distinctions of doctrine are more than verbal games; they can make all the difference in the world as to how life is lived.[39] If nothing else, this indicates that Chesterton took not only his faith but also his theology very seriously. Faith, after all, runs the risk of being mere emotion if it is not backed up by reason. "Theology is only the element of reason in religion, the reason that prevents it from being a mere emotion."[40] It also gives us a hint as to why his conversion was such a gradual process; his "instinctive Christianity" was simply not enough, it had to be thought out very carefully—even though the ultimate affirmation of faith continues to be a "leap," but not a "leap in the dark."

Once Chesterton had passed through the agnosticism of his youth, he became profoundly aware of the very down-to-earth human need for religion, the need he experienced so vividly in himself. This meant, among other things, that he saw atheism not merely as erroneous but as an aberration from "common sense": "It is the reversal of a subconscious assumption in the soul; the sense that there is a meaning and a direction in the world it sees."[41] Far more natural to human experience, in fact, is not the denial of the divine that is atheism but the multiplication of divinities that is paganism. Atheists may, by dint of great efforts, try to show by such studies as comparative religion that all religions are equally fallacious, but what the comparison of religions really shows is that it is simply natural for human beings to crave the supernatural.[42] It is certainly not difficult to show that the history of the human race manifests abundantly this craving. By the same token, however, he argues that, if we look only at the natural arguments for survival, they are all against the survival of the Christian Church. It may be that this is a rather roundabout way of arguing that the survival of the Church founded by Jesus Christ is clearly supernatural, clearly miraculous, but it does get its point across, and it does show that ultimately G. K. Chesterton went the only way he could go, even if it took him a long time to see it as the only way. It is assuredly not without significance that he saw faith and conversion as synonymous; to believe was to turn—to God in Jesus Christ—a constant, not a momentary movement.[43] The turning, however, was not so much a turning away from what was wrong as it was a turning to a realization of what had been right all along: "It is not so much that I have found I was wrong as that I have found why I was right."[44]

There is in faith, not only as Chesterton saw it but also as it happened in him, more than just a hint of mystic vision, a seeing of what rational mind all by itself could not fathom. Not only was he constant in his praise of mysticism, whether the poetical mysticism of Francis of Assisi, the theological mysticism of Thomas Aquinas, or what we might call his own "intellectualistic mysticism," but he saw commitment to Jesus Christ in faith as essentially a mystical venture,[45] which he expresses very strikingly in the image of the infant who is God; reason by itself could never connect divinity and infancy, but the connection is inseparable from Christian faith,[46] which can take us where reason cannot take us—without contradicting reason, and without causing us to make mental somersaults in formulating that faith. Here it is that one can begin to see the aptness of a remark he makes in *Irish Impressions*: "Whenever men are still theological there is still some chance of their being logical."[47] The legacy of the eighteenth and nineteenth centuries, which could see reason only in the form of thoroughly deterministic laws of nature, made the vision that is faith difficult, but it was the task of more than half Chesterton's life to speak up constantly for the vision that is faith, the liberating vision that saw authentic humanity in a responsibility not in thrall to "iron laws," particularly not the "iron economic laws" of British theorists. It was this faith and this vision that enabled him to see life as a pilgrimage which has both a direction and a goal—coming from and leading to God. It was this faith, too, which enabled him to see that what Jesus Christ demanded of his followers was, even though difficult—perhaps next to impossible—not in conflict with reason. "The command of Christ ["turn the other cheek"] is impossible, but it is not insane; it is rather sanity preached to a planet of lunatics."[48] The wisdom of God, after all, is not merely human wisdom.

NOTES

CHAPTER 1

1. Chesterton, "Playing with an Idea," in *The Glass Walking Stick and Other Essays* (London: Methuen, 1955), p. 16.

2. Chesterton, *The Everlasting Man* (Garden City: Doubleday Image Books, 1955), p. 51.

3. Cecil Chesterton, *Gilbert Keith Chesterton: A Criticism* (New York: Lane, 1909), p. x.

4. Chesterton, "The Aim of Education," in *The Spice of Life and Other Essays by G. K. Chesterton*, ed. Dorothy E. Collins (Beaconsfield: Finlayson, 1964), p. 114.

5. Chesterton, *St. Thomas Aquinas* (Garden City: Doubleday Image Books, 1956), p. 113.

6. Maisie Ward, *Return to Chesterton* (New York: Sheed & Ward, 1952), p. 283.

7. Chesterton, *Autobiography* (New York: Sheed & Ward, 1936), p. 23.

8. Christopher Hollis, *The Mind of Chesterton* (Coral Gables: University of Miami Press, 1970), p. 86.

9. Chesterton, *Generally Speaking* (New York: Dodd, Mead, 1979), p. 207.

10. John O'Connor, *Father Brown on Chesterton* (London: Miller, 1937), p. 154.

11. Chesterton, *Autobiography*, p. 342.

12. Quoted in Maisie Ward, *Gilbert Keith Chesterton* (New York: Sheed & Ward, 1943), p. 636.

13. Chesterton, "The Vanity of Vanities," in *G. K. Chesterton: The Apostle and the Wild Ducks and Other Essays*, ed. Dorothy E. Collins (London: Elek Books, 1975), p. 12.

14. Chesterton, *The Resurrection of Rome* (New York: Dodd, Mead, 1930), p. 80.

15. Cecil Chesterton, *Gilbert Keith Chesterton: A Criticism*, p. 112.

16. Chesterton, *Autobiography*, pp. 228–29.

17. Chesterton, "The Blue Cross," in *The Innocence of Father Brown* (London & New York: Cassell, 1911), p. 11.

18. Ian Boyd, "Philosophy in Fiction," in *G. K. Chesterton: A Centenary Appraisal*, ed. John Sullivan (New York: Harper & Row, 1974), p. 42.

19. Ernst Bloch, *Subjekt–Objekt* (Frankfurt am Main: Suhrkamp, 1962), p. 26.

CHAPTER 2

1. Ward, *Gilbert Keith Chesterton*, p. 524.

2. *Daily News* (London), February 13, 1906.

3. Chesterton, *What I Saw in America* (New York: Dodd, Mead, 1922), p. 164.

4. Chesterton, *The Well and the Shallows* (London: Sheed & Ward, 1935), p. 208.

5. Chesterton, *A Handful of Authors* (New York: Sheed & Ward, 1953), p. 163.

6. Plato, *Meno*, 98A; *Theaetetus*, 210C–D.

7. Chesterton, *The New Jerusalem* (London: Hodder & Stoughton, 1920), p. 262.

8. Chesterton, *Autobiography*, p. 180.

9. Chesterton, *Eugenics and Other Evils* (London: Cassell, 1922), p. 164; emphases mine.

10. Neville Braybrooke, "Chesterton Remembered," *The Tablet* (London), December 21, 1928.

11. See Chesterton, *Irish Impressions* (London: Collins, 1919), p. 185.

12. Chesterton, *Robert Louis Stevenson* (New York: Dodd, Mead, 1928), p. 120.

13. Chesterton, *George Bernard Shaw* (New York: Lane, 1909), p. 135.

14. Chesterton, *What's Wrong with the World* (New York: Sheed & Ward, 1956), p. 203.

15. Chesterton, *The Scandal of Father Brown* (New York: Dodd, Mead, 1936), p. 71.

16. Ward, *Gilbert Keith Chesterton*, p. 155.

17. Chesterton, *St. Thomas Aquinas*, p. 144.

18. *The Listener*, December 27, 1934, p. 1086.

19. Ibid., November 14, 1934, p. 836.

20. Chesterton, *Orthodoxy* (Garden City: Doubleday Image Books, 1959), p. 227.

21. *Daily News* (London), December 21, 1906.

22. Chesterton, *George Bernard Shaw*, p. 135.

23. Hugh Kenner, *Paradox in Chesterton* (New York: Sheed & Ward, 1947), p. 126.

24. Chesterton, *A Handful of Authors*, "Ruskin," p. 152.

25. Chesterton, *Charles Dickens* (London: Burns & Oates, 1975), p. 156.

26. Chesterton, *What's Wrong with the World*, p. 127.

27. Chesterton, *Generally Speaking*, p. 9.

28. Chesterton, "The Bigot," in *Lunacy and Letters* (New York: Sheed & Ward, 1958), p. 151.

29. Alzina Stone Dale, *The Outline of Sanity: A Biography of G. K. Chesterton* (Grand Rapids: Eerdmans, 1982), p. 65.

30. Ward, *Gilbert Keith Chesterton*, p. 205.

31. Robert Louis Stevenson, as quoted by Chesterton in *The Glass Walking Stick*, "On the Essay," p. 188.

32. Ibid., p. 189.

33. Chesterton, *The Thing: Why I Am a Catholic* (New York: Dodd, Mead, 1930), p. 210.

34. See Chesterton, *Orthodoxy*, p. 142.

35. Chesterton, *Autobiography*, p. 349.

36. Chesterton, "The Man Who Was Orthodox," *Daily News* (London), June 22, 1907, p. 92.

37. Hilaire Belloc, *On the Place of Gilbert Chesterton in English Letters* (New York: Sheed & Ward, 1940), p. 33.

38. Ward, *Gilbert Keith Chesterton*, p. 204.

39. Ward, *Return to Chesterton*, p. 116.

40. Chesterton, *The Apostle and the Wild Ducks*, "For Persons of the Name of Smith," p. 9.

CHAPTER 3

1. See Chesterton, *St. Thomas Aquinas*, p. 107.

2. See Chesterton, *The Apostle and the Wild Ducks*, pp. 168–69.

3. Chesterton, *The Thing*, p. 4.

4. Chesterton, *George Bernard Shaw*, p. 182.

5. Chesterton, *The Common Man* (London: Sheed & Ward, 1950), p. 93.

6. See Chesterton, *G. F. Watts* (New York: Dutton, 1904), p. 13.

7. See Chesterton, *Orthodoxy*, "The Ethics of Elfland," pp. 46–65.

8. See ibid., p. 50; see also *Fancies vs. Fads* (London: Methuen, 1933), pp. 119–20.

9. Hollis, *The Mind of Chesterton*, p. 36.

10. Chesterton, *Lunacy and Letters*, p. 121.

11. See Chesterton, *Charles Dickens*, p. 109.

12. See Chesterton, *St. Thomas Aquinas*, p. 105.

13. See John Cummings, Introduction to Chesterton, *Charles Dickens*, p. xiv.

14. See ibid., p. ix.

15. See Chesterton, *The End of the Armistice*, comp. F. J. Sheed (London: Sheed & Ward, 1940), pp. 193–95.

16. Chesterton, *Robert Browning* (London: Macmillan, 1903), p. 187.

17. See Chesterton, *Orthodoxy*, p. 90.

18. See ibid., p. 72.

19. Chesterton, *Heretics* (New York: Dodd, Mead, 1923), p. 68.

20. Chesterton, *Charles Dickens*, pp. 142–43.

21. See ibid., p. 5.

22. Richard Baker, "Notes on Chesterton's Notre Dame Lectures on Victorian Literature (10/6/30)," *The Chesterton Review*, 3, No. 2 (1977), 169.

23. Chesterton, *G. F. Watts*, p. 69.

24. Herbert Marshall McLuhan, Introduction to Hugh Kenner, *Paradox in Chesterton*, pp. xxi–xxii.

25. See Chesterton, *Fancies vs. Fads*, pp. 164–65.

26. Chesterton, *What's Wrong with the World*, p. 25.

27. Chesterton, "On the Touchy Realist" in *Avowals and Denials* (New York: Dodd, Mead, 1935), p. 185.

28. Chesterton, "About Modern Girls," in *As I Was Saying* (London: Methuen, 1936), p. 73.

29. See Chesterton, *The Catholic Church and Conversion* (London: Burns & Oates, 1960), p. 92.

30. See Dale, *The Outline of Sanity*, p. 6.

31. Plato, *Euthyphro*, 7A.

32. Ibid., 10A.

33. Chesterton, *Chesterton Essays* (London: Methuen, 1953), pp. 114–15.

34. Aristotle, *Nicomachean Ethics*, 3.4.1113A20–30.

35. Ibid., 3.5.1114B15–25.

36. See Chesterton, *Chesterton on Shakespeare*, ed. Dorothy E. Collins (Henley-on-Thames: Finlayson, 1971), pp. 51–52.

37. See Chesterton, *The End of the Armistice*, pp. 53–54.

38. See ibid., p. 52.

39. Chesterton, *The Glass Walking Stick*, "The Newness of Novelty," p. 165.

40. Ibid.

41. Ibid.

42. See Chesterton, *As I Was Saying*, p. 185.

43. Chesterton, *Eugenics and Other Evils*, p. 52.

44. Ibid.

45. See Chesterton, *On Running After One's Hat and Other Whimsies* (New York: McBride, 1933), pp. 139–41.

46. Chesterton, *William Blake* (New York: Dutton, 1910), p. 160.

47. Chesterton, *Criticisms and Appreciations of Charles Dickens' Work* (New York: Dutton, 1911), p. 14.

48. Chesterton, "On Bright Old Things—and Other Things," in *Sidelights and Other Essays* (London: Sheed & Ward, 1932), p. 6.

49. See *Sidelights*, pp. 31–32, 50.

50. See *Orthodoxy*, p. 10.

51. Chesterton, *Avowals and Denials*, "On Books for Pessimists," pp. 165–66.

52. Ibid., p. 166.

53. Chesterton, *Twelve Types* (London: Humphreys, 1910), p. 26.

54. Chesterton, *The Defendant* (London: Johnson, 1901), p. 8; see also pp. 13–14.

55. See Chesterton, *Robert Browning*, p. 179.

56. See Chesterton, *Charles Dickens*, p. 186.

57. Ward, *Chesterton*, p. 448.

58. See Chesterton, *Autobiography*, p. 99.

59. Chesterton, *A Handful of Authors*, p. 117.

60. Chesterton, *Heretics*, p. 29.

61. Chesterton, *Charles Dickens*, p. 28.

62. See Chesterton, *Alarms and Discursions* (London: Methuen, 1910), pp. 195–96.

63. E. C. Bentley, *Those Days* (London: Constable, 1940), p. 46.

64. Chesterton, *Orthodoxy*, p. 159.

65. Chesterton, *St. Thomas Aquinas*, p. 113.

66. Chesterton, *New Jerusalem*, p. 250.

67. See ibid.

68. See Chesterton, *William Cobbett* (New York: Dodd, Mead, 1925), pp. 141–43.

69. See Chesterton, *A Short History of England* (New York: Lane, 1917), passim.

70. Chesterton, *Chaucer* (London: Faber & Faber, 1932), p. x.

71. Ibid., p. 102.

72. Maureen Corrigan, "Gill, Chesterton and Ruskin: Mediaevalism in the Twentieth Century," *The Chesterton Review*, 9, No. 1 (1983), 26.

73. Chesterton, *The Glass Walking Stick*, p. 185.

74. Chesterton, *The Resurrection of Rome*, p. 21.

CHAPTER 4

1. Chesterton, *William Cobbett*, p. 21.

2. Chesterton, *A Handful of Authors*, p. 98.

3. Chesterton, *Orthodoxy*, p. 34.

4. Chesterton, *The Everlasting Man*, p. 43.

5. See ibid., p. 92.

6. Chesterton, "On Funeral Customs," in *The Selected Essays of G. K. Chesterton*, ed. E. C. Bentley (London: Methuen, 1949), p. 268.

7. Chesterton, *The Everlasting Man*, p. 105.

8. See Chesterton, "On Old Men Who Make Wars," in *All I Survey* (New York: Dodd, Mead, 1933), p. 36.

9. Frank Sheed in Chesterton, *The End of the Armistice*, p. 8 (compiler's note).

10. Chesterton, *William Cobbett*, p. 14.

11. Chesterton, *Fancies vs. Fads*, p. 105.

12. Chesterton, *St. Thomas Aquinas*, p. 161.

13. See Chesterton, *The Everlasting Man*, p. 153.

14. Chesterton, *The Secret of Father Brown* (New York: Penguin, 1975), p. 12.

15. Chesterton, *Eugenics and Other Evils*, pp. 81–82.

16. Chesterton, *St. Thomas Aquinas*, p. 162.

17. See Chesterton, *Chesterton Essays*, "The Wind and Trees," pp. 44–45.

18. See Chesterton, *Heretics*, p. 174.

19. See Chesterton, *Utopia of Usurers* (New York: Boni & Liveright, 1917), pp. 180–81.

20. Chesterton, *The Everlasting Man*, p. 33.

21. Chesterton, *Orthodoxy*, p. 59.

22. See ibid.

23. Chesterton, *Autobiography*, p. 348.

24. Chesterton, *Orthodoxy*, p. 61.

25. See Chesterton, *Utopia of Usurers*, pp. 210–11.

26. Chesterton, "The Free Man," *A Miscellany of Men* (New York: Dodd, Mead, 1912), p. 51.

27. Chesterton, *Orthodoxy*, p. 18.

28. Ibid., p. 25.

29. See Chesterton, *The Thing*, "The Outline of the Fall," pp. 226–27.

30. Chesterton, *All I Survey*, p. 125.

31. Chesterton, *Chaucer*, p. 28.

32. Chesterton, *The Resurrection of Rome*, p. 79.

33. Ibid., p. 81.

34. Chesterton, *The Common Man*, p. 237.

35. Chesterton, *Manalive* (New York: Nelson, 1912), p. 48.

36. Chesterton, *The Thing*, pp. 163–64.

37. See Chesterton, *A Short History of England*, p. 77.

38. See Chesterton, *The Catholic Church and Conversion*, p. 93.

39. Chesterton, *A Miscellany of Men*, p. 78; see also pp. 75–76.

40. See Raymond T. Bond, ed., *The Man Who Was Chesterton* (Garden City: Doubleday Image Books, 1960), pp. 497–98.

41. See Chesterton, *Orthodoxy*, p. 127.

42. Chesterton, *The Everlasting Man*, pp. 25–26.

43. See Chesterton, *Chesterton Essays*, pp. 48–49.

44. See Chesterton, *Orthodoxy*, p. 150.

45. See ibid., p. 128.

46. Stanley L. Jaki, *Chesterton, a Seer of Science* (Urbana and Chicago: University of Illinois Press, 1986).

47. Ibid., p. 15.

1. Chesterton, *Orthodoxy*, p. 47.

2. Chesterton, *Charles Dickens*, p. 6.

3. Chesterton, *The Thing*, p. 44.

4. Chesterton, *All I Survey*, p. 202.

5. Chesterton, "What I Saw in America," in *The Man Who Was Chesterton*, ed. Bond, p. 174.

6. Chesterton, *St. Francis of Assisi* (Garden City: Doubleday Image Books, 1957), p. 97.

7. Chesterton, *Heretics*, p. 268.

8. See Chesterton, *St. Francis of Assisi*, p. 44.

9. Chesterton, *Charles Dickens*, p. 78.

10. Ibid., p. 60.

11. Ibid.

12. See ibid., p. 9.

13. Ibid., p. 16.

14. See "The First Principle," *G. K.'s Weekly*, March 21, 1925, pp. 3–4.

15. Chesterton, *As I Was Saying*, p. 126.

16. Chesterton, *Orthodoxy*, p. 47.

17. Quoted by Dale, *The Outline of Sanity*, p. 262.

18. Margaret Canovan, *G. K. Chesterton: Radical Populist* (New York: Harcourt Brace Jovanovich, 1977), p. 56.

19. Chesterton, *William Cobbett*, p. 41.

20. Chesterton, *Fancies vs. Fads*, p. 215.

21. Chesterton, *What's Wrong with the World*, p. 17.

22. See Chesterton, *Fancies vs. Fads*, p. 85.

23. See Ian Boyd, *The Novels of G. K. Chesterton* (New York: Barnes & Noble, 1975), pp. 6–7, 11.

24. Chesterton, *All Is Grist* (London: Methuen, 1931), p. 22.

25. Ibid., p. 25.

26. Chesterton, *The Superstition of Divorce* (London: Chatto & Windus, 1920), p. 12.

27. See ibid., p. 13.

28. See Chesterton, *The Common Man*, p. 8.

29. See Ward, *Gilbert Keith Chesterton*, pp. 75–78.

30. Chesterton, *Christendom in Dublin* (London: Sheed & Ward, 1932), p. 52.

31. See Chesterton, *The Common Man*, p. 4.

32. See Chesterton, *As I Was Saying*, "About the Workers," pp. 170–71.

33. Chesterton, *What's Wrong with the World*, p. 6.

34. Chesterton, *The Napoleon of Notting Hill* (New York: Lane, 1904), p. 21.

35. See, e.g., Dale, *Outline of Sanity*, pp. 260–61; Ward, *Gilbert Keith Chesterton*, pp. 509–28; Canovan, *G. K. Chesterton: Radical Populist*, pp. 81–96.

36. Hollis, *The Mind of Chesterton*, p. 198.

37. *The Listener*, June 19, 1941.

38. Mario Amadeo, "Chesterton in South America: *What's Wrong with the World* Revisited," *The Chesterton Review*, 2, No. 2 (1976), 262–63.

39. *G. K.'s Weekly*, September 21, 1929, p. 302.

40. Ward, *Gilbert Keith Chesterton*, p. 511.

41. Lawrence J. Clipper, *G. K. Chesterton* (New York: Twayne, 1974), p. 117.

42. "Profit-Sharing and Proportion," *G. K.'s Weekly*, February 11, 1928, p. 961.

43. *The Man Who Was Chesterton*, ed. Bond, pp. 318–19.

44. Ibid., p. 319.

45. Ibid.

46. Chesterton, *The Outline of Sanity* (London: Methuen, 1926), p. 92.

47. Donald Attwater, "The Decline of Distributism," *Commonweal*, 53 (1951), 422.

48. Ward, *Return to Chesterton*, p. 274.

49. Chesterton, *Heretics*, p. 76.

50. Boyd, *The Novels of G. K. Chesterton*, p. 72.

51. See Chesterton, *Eugenics and Other Evils*, p. 18.

52. Chesterton, *The New Jerusalem*, p. 38.

53. See Chesterton, *Robert Louis Stevenson*, pp. 172–73.

54. Chesterton, *The Apostle and the Wild Ducks*, "Tell a Story," p. 49.

55. Chesterton, *Orthodoxy*, p. 28.

56. See ibid., p. 92.

CHAPTER 6

1. Chesterton, *Chaucer*, p. 20.

2. Ibid., p. 21.

3. Ward, *Gilbert Keith Chesterton*, p. 60.

4. Chesterton, *Alarms and Discursions*, pp. 245–46.

5. Chesterton, *What's Wrong with the World*, p. 29.

6. Quentin Lauer, s.j., "Integral Humanism," *Thought*, 57, No. 225 (June 1982), 159.

7. Chesterton, *The Well and the Shallows*, p. 230.

8. Chesterton, *The Everlasting Man*, p. 34; see *Lunacy and Letters*, p. 90.

9. See Chesterton, *A Miscellany of Men*, p. 111.

10. Chesterton, *A Handful of Authors*, p. 78.

11. See Chesterton, *The Thing*, pp. 25–26.

12. Chesterton, *The Everlasting Man*, p. 176.

13. Chesterton, *St. Thomas Aquinas*, p. 36.

14. Ibid., p. 31.

15. Canovan, *G. K. Chesterton: Radical Populist*, p. 29.

16. Chesterton, *All I Survey*, p. 89.

17. Chesterton, *Sidelights*, p. 261.

18. Chesterton, *St. Thomas Aquinas*, p. 37; see also pp. 84, 118.

19. Ibid., p. 39.

20. See Chesterton, *The Thing*, pp. 15–17.

21. Dale, *The Outline of Sanity*, p. 233.

22. Chesterton, *The Common Man*, p. 93.

23. See Chesterton, *The Catholic Church and Conversion*, p. 58.

24. See Chesterton, *The Thing*, "Is Humanism a Religion?," p. 22.

25. Ibid., pp. 13–14.

26. See Chesterton, *The Catholic Church and Conversion*, pp. 111–12.

27. Chesterton, *Lunacy and Letters*, "The Meaning of Dreams," pp. 29–30.

28. Chesterton, *Alarms and Discursions*, p. 189.

29. Chesterton, *Orthodoxy*, p. 86.

30. C. Fred MacRae, "Chesterton and Kipling: Brothers Under the Skin," *The Chesterton Review*, 2, No. 2 (1976), 227.

31. Chesterton, *The Everlasting Man*, p. 113.

32. Ibid., p. 253.

33. See Chesterton, *The Resurrection of Rome*, pp. 150–51.

34. Chesterton, *The Everlasting Man*, p. 254.

35. See Chesterton, *The Catholic Church and Conversion*, p. 126.

36. See Chesterton, *The Everlasting Man*, p. 219.

37. See Chesterton, *Chaucer*, p. 38.

38. Chesterton, *Heretics*, p. 303.

39. See Chesterton, *The Resurrection of Rome*, p. 62.

40. Chesterton, *The Thing*, p. 146.

41. Chesterton, *The Everlasting Man*, p. 168.

42. See ibid., p. 133.

43. See Chesterton, *The Catholic Church and Conversion*, p. 18.

44. Ibid., p. 91.

45. See Chesterton, *The Everlasting Man*, p. 195.

46. See ibid., p. 173.

47. Chesterton, *Irish Impressions*, p. 198.

48. Chesterton, *Varied Types* (New York: Dodd, Mead, 1903), p. 134.

BIBLIOGRAPHY

PRIMARY SOURCES

Alarms and Discursions. London: Methuen, 1910.

All I Survey. New York: Dodd, Mead, 1933.

All Is Grist. London: Methuen, 1931.

As I Was Saying. London: Methuen, 1936.

Autobiography. New York: Sheed & Ward, 1936.

Avowals and Denials. New York: Dodd, Mead, 1935.

The Catholic Church and Conversion. London: Burns & Oates, 1960.

Charles Dickens. London: Methuen, 1906. Repr. London: Burns & Oates, 1975.

Chaucer. London: Faber & Faber, 1932.

Chesterton Essays. London: Methuen, 1953.

Christendom in Dublin. London: Sheed & Ward, 1932.

Chesterton on Shakespeare. Ed. Dorothy E. Collins. Henley-on-Thames: Finlayson, 1971.

The Common Man. London: Sheed & Ward, 1950.

Criticisms and Appreciations of Charles Dickens' Work. New York: Dutton, 1911.

Daily News (London). 2/13/06, 12/21/06, 6/22/07.

The Defendant. London: Johnson, 1901.

The End of the Armistice. Compiled by F. J. Sheed. London and New York: Sheed & Ward, 1940.

Eugenics and Other Evils. London: Cassell, 1922.

The Everlasting Man. London: Hodder & Stoughton, 1925. Repr. Garden City: Doubleday Image Books, 1955.

Fancies vs. Fads. London: Methuen, 1933.

Generally Speaking. New York: Dodd, Mead, 1979.

George Bernard Shaw. New York: Lane, 1909.

G. F. Watts. New York: Dutton, 1904.

G. K. Chesterton: The Apostle and the Wild Ducks and Other Essays. Ed. Dorothy E. Collins. London: Elek Books, 1975.

G. K.'s Weekly. 3/21/25, 2/11/28, 9/21/29.

The Glass Walking Stick and Other Essays. London: Methuen, 1955.

A Handful of Authors. New York: Sheed & Ward, 1953.

Heretics. New York: John Lane, 1905. Repr. New York: Dodd, Mead, 1923.

The Innocence of Father Brown. London and New York: Cassell, 1911.

Irish Impressions. London: Collins, 1919.

The Listener. 11/14/34, 12/27/34, 6/19/41.

Lunacy and Letters. New York: Sheed & Ward, 1958.

Manalive. New York: Nelson, 1912.

A Miscellany of Men. New York: Dodd, Mead, 1912.

The Napoleon of Notting Hill. New York: Lane, 1904.

The New Jerusalem. London: Hodder & Stoughton, 1920.

On Running After One's Hat and Other Whimsies. New York: McBride, 1933.

Orthodoxy. New York: Dodd, Mead, 1908. Repr. Garden City: Doubleday Image Books, 1959.

The Outline of Sanity. London: Methuen, 1926.

The Resurrection of Rome. New York: Dodd, Mead, 1930.

Robert Browning. London: Macmillan, 1903.

Robert Louis Stevenson. New York: Dodd, Mead, 1928.

St. Francis of Assisi. London: Hodder & Stoughton, 1923. Repr. Garden City: Doubleday Image Books, 1957.

St. Thomas Aquinas. London: Hodder & Stoughton, 1933. Repr. Garden City: Doubleday Image Books, 1956.

The Scandal of Father Brown. New York: Dodd, Mead, 1936.

The Secret of Father Brown. New York: Penguin, 1975.

A Short History of England. New York: Lane, 1917.

Sidelights and Other Essays. London: Sheed & Ward, 1932.

The Spice of Life and Other Essays by G. K. Chesterton. Ed. Dorothy E. Collins. Beaconsfield: Finlayson, 1964.

The Superstition of Divorce. London: Chatto & Windus, 1920.

The Thing: Why I Am a Catholic. New York: Dodd, Mead, 1930.

Twelve Types. London: Humphreys, 1910.

Utopia of Usurers. New York: Boni & Liveright, 1917.

Varied Types. New York: Dodd, Mead, 1903.

The Well and the Shallows. London: Sheed & Ward, 1935.

What I Saw in America. New York: Dodd, Mead, 1922.

What's Wrong with the World. New York: Sheed & Ward, 1956.

William Blake. New York: Dutton, 1910.

William Cobbett. New York: Dodd, Mead, 1925.

SELECTED SECONDARY SOURCES

Amadeo, Mario. "Chesterton in South America: *What's Wrong with the World* Revisited," *The Chesterton Review*, 2, No. 2 (1976), 260–66.

Aristotle. *Nicomachean Ethics*.

Attwater, Donald. "The Decline of Distributism," *Commonweal*, 53 (2/2/51), 421–22.

Baker, Richard. "Notes on Chesterton's Notre Dame Lectures on Victorian Literature (10/6/30),"*The Chesterton Review*, 3, No. 2 (1977), 165–67.

Belloc, Hilaire. *On the Place of Gilbert Chesterton in English Letters*. New York: Sheed & Ward, 1940.

Bentley, E. C. *Those Days*. London: Constable, 1940.

—— (ed.). *The Selected Essays of G. K. Chesterton*. London: Methuen, 1949.

Bloch, Ernst. *Subjekt–Objekt*. Frankfurt am Main: Suhrkamp, 1962.

Bond, Raymond T. (ed.). *The Man Who Was Chesterton*. Garden City: Doubleday Image Books, 1960.

Boyd, Ian. "Philosophy in Fiction" in *G. K. Chesterton: A Centenary Appraisal*. Ed. John Sullivan. New York: Harper & Row, 1974. Pp. 40–57.

——. *The Novels of G. K. Chesterton*. New York: Barnes & Noble, 1975.

Braybrooke, Neville. "Chesterton Remembered," in *The Tablet* (London), December 21, 1928.

Canovan, Margaret. *G. K. Chesterton: Radical Populist*. New York: Harcourt Brace Jovanovich, 1977.

Chesterton, Cecil. *Gilbert Keith Chesterton: A Criticism*. New York: Lane, 1909.

Clipper, Lawrence J. *G. K. Chesterton*. New York: Twayne, 1974.

Corrigan, Maureen. "Gill, Chesterton and Ruskin: Mediaevalism in the Twentieth Century," *The Chesterton Review*, 9, No. 1 (1983), 15–30.

Dale, Alzina Stone. *The Outline of Sanity: A Biography of G. K. Chesterton*. Grand Rapids: Eerdmans, 1982.

Hollis, Christopher. *The Mind of Chesterton*. Coral Gables: University of Miami Press, 1970.

Jaki, Stanley L. *Chesterton, a Seer of Science*. Urbana and Chicago: University of Illinois Press, 1986.

Kenner, Hugh. *Paradox in Chesterton*. New York: Sheed & Ward, 1947.

Lauer, Quentin, s.j. "Integral Humanism," *Thought*, 57, No. 225 (June 1982), 157–64.

MacRae, C. Fred. "Chesterton and Kipling: Brothers Under the Skin," *The Chesterton Review*, 2, No. 2 (1976), 226–39.

O'Connor, John. *Father Brown on Chesterton*. London: Miller, 1937.

Plato. *Euthyphro. Meno. Theaetetus.*

Sullivan, John (ed.). *G. K. Chesterton: Centenary Appraisal*. New York: Harper & Row, 1974.

Ward, Maisie. *Gilbert Keith Chesterton*. New York: Sheed & Ward, 1943.

——. *Return to Chesterton*. New York: Sheed & Ward, 1952.

INDICES

INDEX NOMINUM

Amadeo, Mario, 133
Aquinas, St. Thomas, 7, 9, 12, 18, 37,
   41, 70, 80, 81, 140, 154, 166
Archimedes, 84
Aristotle, 3, 7, 9, 37, 41, 57, 68, 70, 84
Arnold, Matthew, 62

Bach, J. S., 73
Bacon, Francis, 9
Baring, Maurice, 6
Belloc, Hilaire, 6, 49, 50
Bentley, E. C., 50, 80
Berkeley, George, 9
Blake, William, 6, 70
Bloch, Ernst, 23
Bonaventure, St., 7
Boyd, Ian, 23, 123, 143
Braybrooke, Neville, 33
Browning, Robert, 3, 6, 60, 70, 78
Byron, George, 59

Canovan, Margaret, 132, 154
Chaucer, Geoffrey, 6, 70, 81, 82, 140,
   149
Chesterton, Cecil, 50
Clemens, Cyril, 16, 50
Clipper, Lawrence, 135
Cobbett, William, 91, 121

Dale, Alzina, 42, 66, 132, 156
Dante, 81, 116, 140
Darwin, Charles, 86, 109
Dawson, Christopher, 6
Descartes, René, 7, 9
Dewey, John, 109
Dickens, Charles, 6, 39, 70, 78, 79, 112
Doyle, Arthur Conan, 93

Eddington, Arthur, 109
Einstein, Albert, 84, 109
Eliot, T. S., 38, 119
Emerson, Ralph Waldo, 46

Fabre, Jean Henri, 109
Feuerbach, Ludwig, 108

Francis of Assisi, St., 6, 18, 61, 70, 81,
   114, 140, 166
Freud, Sigmund, 147

Gardner, Martin, 109, 110

Hardy, Thomas, 59
Hegel, G. W. F., 5, 7, 10, 11, 18, 46,
   47, 48, 55, 88, 103, 153
Hobbes, Thomas, 9
Hollis, Christopher, 14, 132
Homer, 145
Hume, David, 3, 9, 48, 55, 93
Huxley, Aldous and Julian, 109

Ibsen, Henrik, 29
Ingersoll, Robert, 113
Isaacs, Godfrey and Rufus, 142

Jaki, Stanley, 109, 110
Jefferson, Thomas, 113
Jesus Christ, 60, 153, 154, 156, 163,
   165, 166
Johnson, Samuel, 3

Kant, Immanuel, 7, 10, 55, 153
Kenner, Hugh, 39, 63
Kierkegaard, Søren, 7, 10
Knox, Ronald A., 25, 133

Lawrence, D. H., 60
Locke, John, 9, 93

Marconi, Guglielmo, 142
Marx, Karl, 10, 108, 129, 130, 135,
   136, 147
Maugham, W. Somerset, 60
McLuhan, Marshall, 62
Mussolini, Benito, 130

Nagel, Ernest, 109
Newman, John Henry, 11, 163
Nietzsche, Friedrich, 10, 14, 108, 115,
   147

O'Connor, John, 16, 50
Oppenheimer, Robert, 109

Plato, 7, 9, 29, 37, 58, 66, 67, 70, 116

Remarque, Erich Maria, 59, 60
Rodin, François, 73
Rousseau, Jean Jacques, 46
Rubens, Peter Paul, 145
Ruskin, John, 139

Sartre, Jean-Paul, 108, 147
Shakespeare, William, 58, 70, 73, 145
Shaw, George Bernard, 6, 29, 34, 39, 45, 54, 55
Shelley, Percy Bysshe, 58, 59
Smith, Adam, 123, 128

Socrates, 57, 58, 67, 68
Spinoza, Baruch, 7, 9
Stevenson, Robert Louis, 6, 33, 42
Suthers, R. B., 100
Swinburne, Algernon, 59

Thackeray, William Makepeace, 3
Titterton, William, 50

Van Gogh, Vincent, 73

Ward, Maisie, 3, 14, 16, 38, 42, 50, 51, 65, 78, 128, 132, 134, 139
Wells, H. G., 6, 21, 45, 87
Whitehead, Alfred North, 5, 109
Whitman, Walt, 58

INDEX RERUM

aberrations, 89

absolute, 64, 103, 126; absolutely, 27, 64, 74, 144

abstract, 57, 59, 60, 108, 111, 112, 124, 130, 149, 162; abstraction, 149

action, 14, 15, 26, 49, 58, 70, 71, 74, 105, 129, 130, 138, 141, 148; activity, 47, 52, 53, 54, 63, 66, 99, 144, 150

adversaries, 29, 56

aesthetic, 20, 65, 69, 88

affirmation, 16, 26, 41, 47, 68, 153, 162, 164

agent, 86, 148

agnostic, 93, 95, 157, 160; agnosticism, 28, 111, 160, 165

agree, 25, 60, 94, 104, 123; agreement, 9, 73, 75

analysis, 41; analytically, 42

anarchy, 76

angels, 155

Anglo-Saxon, 55, 93

answer, 3, 10, 12, 17, 28, 29, 36, 41, 42, 44, 54, 56, 58, 72, 80, 81, 84, 85, 90, 109, 128, 151, 156

anthropology, 94; anthropologists, 93, 95

anti-Semitism, 141, 143

apologete, 45, 158; apologetics, 6, 50

arbitrary, 17, 68, 107, 122; arbitrariness, 16, 17, 64, 87, 104, 142

architecture, 81, 104

argument, 10, 22, 29, 41, 50, 59, 72, 77, 78, 86, 89, 100, 142, 165; argumentation, 22, 44

Aristotelian, 69, 146

art, 47, 65, 69, 70, 81, 82, 83, 91, 111, 112, 145, 152, 161; artist, 23, 69, 96, 98, 111, 148; artistic, 81, 82, 88, 107, 115, 145

artificial, 9, 147, 164

articulate, 53; articulation, 47

atheist, 21, 33, 157, 165; atheistic, 129, 130, 131

attitude, 23, 69, 74, 86, 106, 114, 124, 142, 143, 144, 148, 157

authentic, 12, 35, 50, 80, 85, 90, 94, 103, 119, 149, 150, 157, 159, 166; authentically, 19, 85, 103, 133, 147, 148, 162

authority, 29, 54, 154, 162, 163; authoritative, 66, 104, 163

autobiography, 8; autobiographical, 8, 112

awareness, 16, 29, 32, 73, 90, 96, 111, 147, 155

axiological, 147

bad, 52, 53, 54, 68, 70, 75, 92

basic, 37, 38, 62, 71, 80, 126, 128

beauty, 70, 149; beautiful, 78

behavior, 63, 65, 85, 88, 89, 90, 99

being, 15, 16, 19, 20, 24, 47, 52, 67, 92, 99, 107, 112, 114, 115, 148, 152, 153, 155; beings, 10, 49, 52, 53, 54, 56, 59, 63, 64, 74, 84, 92, 98, 101, 111, 112, 114, 115, 120, 122, 123, 125, 135, 136, 138, 141, 148, 149, 152, 154, 156, 157, 159

Being, 16, 97, 154

belief, 20, 30, 32, 33, 34, 40, 44, 48, 61, 106, 108, 123, 131, 154, 162, 163

believe, 20, 21, 27, 30, 32, 33, 34, 35, 39, 40, 46, 47, 48, 49, 92, 94, 100, 101, 106, 107, 113, 129, 143, 146, 153, 162, 165; believing, 10, 48, 49, 108, 162

birth control, 29, 126, 164

Black, 143, 148

body, 92, 155, 159

breed, 63, 89, 122, 123; breeding, 74, 122

brilliance, 23, 38

bureaucracy, 114, 118, 120, 131

Calvinists, 102

capitalism, 90, 117, 128, 130, 131, 133, 136; capitalist, 24, 54, 90, 114, 121, 135

Catholic, 4, 19, 23, 30, 56, 81, 102, 103, 104, 108, 155, 156, 157, 158, 162, 163; Catholicism, 45, 66, 81, 103, 104, 156, 157, 158

cause, 61, 67, 78, 120, 143

certain, 29, 30, 41, 54, 57, 84, 114, 134, 144; certainty, 11, 28, 29, 30, 32, 40, 56, 57, 99

challenge, 43, 84

change, 40, 41, 72, 73, 74, 75, 76, 86, 108, 138, 144, 153

chaos, 14, 76
character, 8, 42, 54, 68, 69, 78, 89,
138, 161; characteristic, 23, 50, 62,
63, 89, 148
choice, 39, 49, 64, 68, 77, 100, 101,
102, 126, 127
choose, 43, 99, 103, 117; choosing, 71,
103, 125; chosen, 47
Christian, 6, 19, 21, 45, 68, 86, 98,
119, 127, 128, 129, 146, 147, 149,
150, 152, 153, 154, 156, 157, 161,
163, 165, 166; Christianity, 103,
108, 128, 129, 153, 154, 160, 164
Church, 14, 30, 81, 102, 103, 105, 108,
155, 156, 157, 160, 161, 162, 163,
164, 165
civilization, 82, 102, 112
claim, 29, 35, 41, 45, 46, 57, 58, 87,
88, 92, 107, 108, 109, 120, 122, 157,
163
cleverness, 32, 121, 144
collectivism, 90, 117, 130
commitment, 26, 129, 161, 162, 166
common, 11, 13, 37, 51, 84, 106, 114,
115, 116, 128, 129, 149, 159
common sense, 11, 37, 46, 57, 74, 82,
106, 113, 116, 131, 159, 163, 165
communicate, 82, 115; communication, 70, 82
communism, 117, 129, 130, 136
community, 46
compromise, 61
concept, 11, 46, 55, 63, 66, 67, 70, 73,
74, 76, 88, 100, 146, 156, 161
concern, 8, 54, 62, 64, 111, 118, 128,
134
conclusion, 14, 18, 19, 43, 53, 68, 88,
110, 158; conclude, 64, 161
concrete, 36, 71, 75, 90, 94, 111, 112,
117, 119, 120, 126, 131, 133; concretely, 64, 105, 131, 132, 156
condition, 13, 64, 80, 105, 118, 123,
128
conduct, 28, 29, 46, 62
confidence, 27, 85
connection, 18, 81, 109, 118, 166
connotations, 12, 75
conscience, 119, 156
consciousness, 7, 95, 145, 151, 156,
163
consistently, 7, 10, 14, 56, 100, 123
constant, 9, 12, 17, 26, 28, 30, 35, 53,
61, 72, 73, 76, 81, 107, 121
content, 46, 59, 63, 76, 111, 161

contention, 3, 47, 80, 101, 150
continuous, 48, 77
contradiction, 30, 32, 34, 75, 85, 96,
99, 145, 146; contradictory, 50, 75
controversy, 1, 141
conversation, 50, 112
conversion, 30, 45, 66, 81, 82, 103,
128, 155, 156, 158, 164, 165; convert, 29, 40, 104, 157, 163
conviction, 17, 18, 19, 20, 21, 29, 35,
37, 38, 44, 45, 46, 47, 56, 57, 58, 62,
64, 71, 73, 76, 78, 84, 94, 111, 112,
113, 117, 123, 127, 128, 129, 135,
143, 150, 158, 159, 161, 162, 163;
convince, 11, 12, 20, 21, 28, 33, 39,
40, 41, 44, 52, 56, 59, 61, 70, 76, 78,
82, 84, 85, 103, 108, 112, 131; convincing, 38
copy, 37, 75
cosmos, 21, 26, 98
courage, 34, 57, 63, 104, 143, 155, 159
courtesy, 114
covenant, 127
create, 59, 75, 96, 107, 152, 155; creative, 96, 144, 150, 152, 155; creativity, 88, 97, 99, 107, 111
creation, 59, 75, 82, 96, 98, 105, 108,
125, 161
Creation, 113
Creator, 59, 113, 150
creed, 108, 113, 162, 163
crime, 120, 121
criterion, 68, 75, 150
criticism, 1, 23, 31, 50, 88, 123, 128;
critical, 35, 61, 82, 124
cult, 23, 25
culture, 64, 68, 72, 81, 91, 121, 124,
148; cultivation, 150; cultural, 40,
64
custom, 69, 87
cynic, 78, 117, 127, 151

decision, 58, 101
deduce, 10; deduction, 10, 41
define, 23, 74, 104; definition, 55, 57,
131, 151; definitive, 28, 29, 61, 164
democracy, 112, 113, 114, 115, 117,
118, 154; democratic, 113, 118, 154
demonstration, 22; demonstrable, 11
dependence, 18, 148
descriptive, 35, 36, 52, 87; descriptions, 86
determining, 63, 129
determinism, 93, 100, 102, 110; de-

terminist, 100; deterministic, 99, 166

develop, 50, 108; development, 87, 125, 134, 148, 150, 164

dialectic, 23, 92; dialectical, 48, 55

dignity, 85, 101, 106, 112, 115, 120, 133, 147, 148, 151, 157

dimensions, 70, 111

direction, 73, 166

discipline, 10, 55, 164

discussion, 30, 75, 87

distinction, 10, 45, 47, 52, 53, 67, 82, 89, 92, 104, 105, 155, 159, 164; distinguish, 57, 135

distributism, 90, 131, 133, 134, 136, 138, 139, 140, 141; distributist, 131, 132, 133, 137, 139, 140, 141

divine, 46, 99, 107, 108, 113, 114, 123, 125, 131, 135, 147, 148, 153, 154, 155, 156; divinity, 60, 123, 153, 157, 159, 166

divorce, 29, 126, 127

doctrine, 59, 112, 133, 153, 160, 164

dogma, 21, 39, 56, 94, 103, 113, 144, 163, 164; dogmatic, 32, 39, 56, 107, 108; dogmatism, 108; dogmatist, 39, 86

doubt, 11, 34, 56, 57, 77, 79, 94, 95

drawings, 86, 87, 88

dualism, 89, 159

duty, 48, 70, 153

economic, 69, 71, 111, 125, 130, 131, 134, 137, 139, 166

education, 63, 64, 120, 124, 126

Edwardian, 43, 61, 62, 87

emotional, 14, 40, 45, 100, 102, 108, 113, 114, 160, 162, 164

end, 53, 54, 105, 152, 153

England, 31, 61, 87, 115, 117, 119, 123, 128, 139, 143, 144, 156, 161

English, 1, 2, 6, 9, 20, 39, 62, 80, 81, 91, 104, 117, 122, 128, 143, 156, 163

Enlightenment, 27, 82, 85, 147

enthusiasm, 1, 39, 43, 45, 49, 78, 130, 158, 163

equal, 112, 113, 114, 115, 118, 143, 144, 154, 162; equality, 113, 114, 115, 117, 143, 144, 154

essay, 2, 5, 25

essential, 17, 35, 64, 78, 112, 125, 133, 148, 151

establishment, 22, 55, 105

ethics, 62, 69; ethical, 20, 66

etymology, 69

Eucharist, 155

eugenics, 63, 88, 110, 121, 122; eugenicists, 74

evaluate, 29; evaluation, 75, 76

evidence, 34, 35, 86, 87, 110, 141

evil, 47, 52, 53, 54, 57, 58, 59, 61, 69, 70, 74, 77, 78, 79, 100, 101, 120, 123, 127, 139

evolution, 73, 86, 87, 88, 122; evolutionary, 87; evolutionist, 86, 110, 150

excitement, 12, 17, 43

exemplar, 36, 75, 76

existence, 12, 16, 17, 18, 32, 33, 47, 58, 75, 78, 79, 80, 100, 101, 106, 107, 119, 126, 128, 143, 147; exist, 12, 48, 53, 66, 129, 154

experience, 14, 16, 18, 47, 55, 69, 72, 79, 141, 157, 162, 165; experiences, 17, 79, 80, 84

experiment, 2, 89, 132

express, 3, 10, 12, 18, 33, 38, 43, 70, 82, 89, 123, 127, 166; expression, 13, 23, 38, 42, 43, 159

fact, 3, 10, 21, 67, 69, 78, 100, 102, 109, 113, 115, 135, 136, 139, 158

fairy, 58, 97, 98

faith, 20, 21, 30, 34, 45, 62, 66, 104, 107, 118, 148, 149, 158, 160, 162, 164, 165, 166

Fall, the, 59

fallacious, 87, 165

family, 115, 125, 127, 144, 156

Fascism, 130

fault, 66, 81, 86, 121

fiction, 101, 116

finite, 30, 94

force, 69, 86, 87

form, 31, 39, 68, 77

formulate, 36, 41, 161

foundation, 27, 29, 58, 66, 127

free, 16, 21, 52, 53, 64, 78, 95, 99, 100, 101, 103, 105, 106, 117, 138, 146, 154

freedom, 30, 43, 59, 90, 94, 99, 101, 102, 103, 104, 105, 106, 130, 132, 134, 137, 155, 162

Freudian, 70

fundamental, 6, 12, 14, 71, 80, 163

future, 65, 71, 102, 158, 164

generalization, 64, 72, 157

genetic, 74, 88, 89

genius, 2, 3, 4, 17, 81
gift, 7, 16, 17, 18, 50, 80, 97, 101, 112, 113, 147, 155
goal, 8, 77, 124, 125, 134, 150, 166
God, 7, 14, 16, 17, 18, 44, 45, 46, 47, 52, 59, 61, 86, 87, 95, 96, 97, 98, 101, 104, 107, 108, 112, 125, 129, 143, 147, 148, 150, 151, 152, 153, 154, 155, 159, 161, 162, 165, 166
good, 15, 16, 27, 41, 52, 53, 54, 57, 58, 59, 60, 61, 68, 70, 71, 75, 77, 78, 79, 92, 98, 100, 105, 150; goodness, 16, 52, 53, 58, 59, 68, 89
Gothic, 14, 81, 140
grateful, 7, 16, 17, 97; gratitude, 16, 17, 18, 97, 98, 113
gratuitous, 17, 72
greatness, 107, 112, 145
greed, 24, 118
ground, 21, 27, 29, 30, 41, 97, 107, 108, 163
growth, 73, 91, 125, 135
guarantee, 30, 31, 57, 68, 73, 105

happy, 70, 72, 80, 118
health, 159
healthy, 27, 61, 159
heritage, 89, 140, 149, 161
hero, 114, 122, 159
history, 7, 37, 76, 81, 84, 87, 101, 102, 139, 149, 160, 165
honest, 23, 45, 69
humanism, 146, 147, 148, 149, 150, 151, 155, 157
humanity, 60, 91, 106, 111, 112, 117, 119, 121, 123, 133, 134, 149, 154; humanize, 84, 133, 134
humor, 22, 50
hypostatic union, 30
hypothesis, 87; hypothetical, 44

idea, 7, 8, 14, 15, 16, 25, 32, 36, 37, 47, 50, 62, 75, 76, 87, 114, 119, 123, 132, 133, 138, 151, 157
ideal, 36, 73, 75, 76, 77, 78, 90, 114, 117, 118, 123, 124, 132, 133, 134, 137, 141, 150, 161; idealist, 36, 76, 109, 117; idealizing, 76
ideology, 89
illegitimate, 87, 88
illustrate, 22, 75, 104; illustration, 22, 25

image, 75, 96, 98, 112, 114, 150, 152, 154, 166
imagination, 9, 39
immoral, 66, 68, 69, 88, 89
implication, 3, 71, 122, 132
imply, 56, 117, 128, 130, 161
important, 10, 12, 13, 26, 32, 34, 37, 53, 55, 57, 58, 62, 63, 73, 79, 81, 84, 85, 87, 89, 97, 99, 100, 118, 119, 125, 132, 150, 154, 159, 164
improvement, 2, 71, 72, 74, 128, 131, 135, 138, 145
incarnate, 46
Incarnation, 153, 155
incompatible, 44, 106, 121
independent, 65, 104, 161
indignant, 69, 77
individual, 46, 62, 64, 68, 88, 89, 91, 95, 104, 105, 106, 111, 119, 133, 148, 149, 153, 156; individualism, 27
indubitably, 55, 56
industrial, 121, 128, 130, 132, 133
inevitable, 19, 20, 91, 100, 101; inevitably, 9, 16, 32, 44, 49, 64, 72, 144, 145
infallible, 29, 57, 72, 85, 162, 164
infer, 41, 92
infinite, 17, 30, 48, 107, 153
influence, 4, 25, 26, 37, 144, 153
initiative, 8, 148
inquiry, 17, 19, 35, 149
insane, 35, 48, 56, 134
insight, 69, 90, 110, 114, 121
instinct, 11, 17, 41, 42, 125, 164
institution, 23, 103, 124, 125, 127
integrality, 151, 155; integrity, 77, 151
intellect, 45, 64, 112, 160; intellectual, 14, 38, 45, 57, 78, 84, 87, 96, 104, 111, 132, 133, 134, 160; intellectually, 25, 46, 49, 128; intellectuals, 162
intelligent, 23, 35, 50, 51, 96, 115, 137; intelligence, 89; intelligentsia, 39
intelligible, 30, 32, 34, 38, 41, 76, 101, 108, 114, 137
intend, 4, 38, 53, 88
intention, 53, 98, 148
interesting, 50, 51, 54, 58
interpret, 41, 69; interpretation, 70, 87
interrelated, 91, 92

irrational, 10, 34, 35, 38, 57, 144
irresponsible, 15
issue, 5, 6, 29, 31, 40, 43, 75, 90

Jesuit, 1, 2, 4
Jew, 102, 141, 142, 143, 159
journalism, 46, 65, 111; journalist, 3, 4, 5, 24, 65
joy, 79, 80
judge, 31, 64, 68, 73, 124; judging, 28, 67, 75
judgment, 35, 44, 58, 60, 65, 68, 69, 70, 74, 75, 76, 89, 94
justice, 117, 129
justify, 35, 46, 67; justifiably, 36, 40, 58, 72; justification, 3, 29, 34, 36, 96

know, 2, 4, 7, 12, 15, 17, 18, 25, 32, 34, 39, 43, 46, 50, 53, 55, 56, 57, 61, 63, 64, 67, 69, 70, 72, 74, 79, 84, 87, 89, 94, 95, 96, 114, 131, 133, 162; knowing, 7, 34, 49, 55, 57, 61, 64, 99, 131; knowledge, 9, 12, 28, 29, 30, 37, 47, 63, 64, 85

language, 33, 38, 40, 52, 57, 104, 141, 155
law, 34, 35, 36, 61, 65, 87, 103, 104, 106, 113, 118, 119, 120, 129, 137, 138, 151, 153, 166
legal, 65, 119, 127, 135
legislation, 141
legitimate, 55, 85, 86, 88, 91, 110, 142; legitimize, 46
liberal, 130
liberation, 103
liberty, 39, 99, 102, 104, 106, 120, 140, 155, 163
life, 3, 8, 12, 14, 15, 16, 17, 18, 20, 21, 26, 27, 28, 29, 30, 34, 43, 45, 46, 48, 49, 51, 54, 55, 57, 61, 62, 67, 77, 78, 79, 80, 99, 100, 101, 107, 111, 113, 125, 127, 132, 133, 134, 139, 147, 150, 151, 155, 158, 163, 164, 166
linguistic, 55
literary, 1, 3, 6, 23, 50, 69, 70, 111
literature, 6, 62, 65
living, 25, 28, 35, 43, 49, 52, 71, 72
logic, 16, 27, 39, 43, 75, 92, 96, 106, 113; logical, 10, 19, 20, 22, 27, 33, 39, 41, 72, 100, 106, 149, 166; logician, 96
love, 12, 50, 60, 78, 112, 113, 114, 118, 132, 149, 157; lovable, 60, 112, 157; loving, 60, 78, 115

machine, 47, 54, 73, 91, 134, 148; machinery, 54, 134, 137
man, 8, 14, 17, 18, 26, 30, 35, 36, 40, 49, 50, 51, 61, 78, 80, 84, 86, 93, 95, 96, 98, 99, 101, 104, 112, 113, 114, 115, 119, 124, 125, 131, 133, 134, 135, 145, 146, 149, 150, 152, 153, 154, 155, 158
marriage, 113, 125, 126, 127, 164
Marxist, 23, 129, 130, 136
Mass, 25, 155
material, 36, 76, 89, 101, 107, 124, 132, 134, 136, 159; materialism, 108, 124; materialist, 21, 32, 34, 67, 93, 108, 110
mathematics, 35; mathematical, 11, 16, 36, 81, 85
matter, 47, 49, 76, 89, 92, 107, 135, 155
mean, 12, 13, 15, 27, 28, 33, 34, 36, 39, 42, 47, 49, 53, 55, 57, 61, 64, 68, 69, 73, 86, 100, 103, 110, 112, 113, 114, 115, 116, 119, 125, 141, 145, 146, 147, 150, 151
    meaning, 12, 13, 21, 27, 28, 32, 33, 42, 44, 48, 77, 78, 93, 102, 104, 161, 164, 165; meaningful, 55, 66, 71, 73, 150, 162; meaningless, 18, 57, 64, 73, 150, 162
medieval, 38, 45, 65, 80, 81, 82, 104, 133, 139, 140, 148, 161; medievalism, 76, 139
men, 23, 39, 48, 60, 81, 88, 102, 104, 108, 111, 113, 118, 129, 143, 144, 154, 155, 158
mental, 65, 66, 125
message, 11, 64, 102, 133, 156
metaphor, 13, 16, 36, 93, 97
metaphysics, 109, 110; metaphysical, 20, 37, 63, 101, 124
method, 48, 92, 110
Middle Ages, 76, 80, 81, 82, 133, 139, 140, 148
mind, 3, 4, 7, 8, 11, 14, 20, 21, 28, 29, 31, 32, 36, 37, 38, 44, 47, 48, 57, 62, 63, 70, 78, 80, 82, 85, 87, 93, 97, 100, 102, 104, 105, 107, 108, 115, 116, 130, 149, 157, 166
minority, 23, 119, 129, 131, 144, 156
miracle, 16, 17, 21, 101, 108, 112, 155; miraculous, 32, 95, 108, 165

model, 75, 124, 139, 154
modern, 32, 40, 66, 76, 83, 104, 106, 118, 121, 127, 133, 134, 154, 156, 158; modernity, 83
monasticism, 81
money, 119, 121, 134, 135
monopoly, 136, 142
moral, 5, 6, 29, 35, 42, 43, 44, 49, 52, 53, 57, 58, 61, 64, 65, 66, 67, 68, 69, 70, 71, 74, 75, 76, 89, 93, 94, 99, 111, 114, 121, 125, 133; morally, 57, 64, 65, 66; morality, 61, 62, 65, 66, 68, 69, 70, 71, 91
mystery, 16, 32, 43, 56, 145, 151; mysteries, 21, 46, 85, 152; mysterious, 32, 152, 155
mystical, 16, 17, 32, 42, 43, 54, 135, 136, 145, 166
myth, 63; mythological, 159, 161; mythology, 98

natural, 9, 19, 20, 21, 33, 40, 47, 52, 53, 54, 67, 80, 101, 106, 108, 115, 122, 135, 137, 152, 157, 158, 165; naturalism, 21, 32, 73, 97, 106, 107, 147
nature, 16, 19, 20, 21, 22, 35, 36, 47, 53, 54, 59, 70, 80, 92, 93, 97, 98, 106, 107, 115, 124, 125, 141, 144, 151, 154, 166
Nazi, 74, 89, 121, 122
necessary, 1, 9, 10, 30, 44, 52, 74, 87, 95, 102, 129, 154, 158; necessarily, 1, 21, 43, 48, 56, 67, 71, 72, 73, 121; necessity, 21, 85, 91, 164
need, 10, 16, 17, 22, 40, 44, 47, 86, 87, 89, 91, 118, 119, 125, 132, 158, 159
nonsense, 13, 70, 87, 97, 106
notion, 71, 72, 76, 160

object, 11, 14, 21, 34, 66, 112
objective, 19, 44, 46, 65, 68, 162; objectively, 31, 65, 69, 70; objectivity, 68, 69, 82
opinion, 22, 27, 29, 30, 40, 41, 72, 84, 115, 116, 164
opposition, 24, 70, 87, 121, 144
optimism, 35, 78, 84; optimist, 52, 58
order, 47, 76, 113, 140, 145
ordinary, 10, 17, 28, 51, 56, 60, 112, 113, 115, 116, 117, 139, 145
organism, 63, 87, 89, 148
orientation, 52, 73, 149

origin, 108, 113, 125; original, 16, 33, 80
orthodox, 86
ought, 15, 16, 17, 61, 64, 65, 67, 75, 146
ownership, 54, 90, 128, 131, 136, 137, 139

pacifism, 29, 59, 60
pagan, 153, 155, 158; paganism, 108, 155, 156, 159, 165
paradigm, 76
paradox, 22, 26, 30, 31, 32, 33, 38, 39, 50, 100; paradoxical, 9, 22, 23, 25, 27, 28, 30, 34, 42, 43, 46, 48, 57, 58
particular, 37, 50, 68; particulars, 36, 75
peasant, 121, 134, 139
perception, 11, 63
permanent, 75, 76, 80, 127
person, 11, 15, 16, 18, 23, 26, 46, 49, 50, 52, 66, 67, 68, 69, 70, 89, 94, 124, 148, 151, 153, 162; personal, 2, 16, 17, 49, 86, 97, 107, 118, 120, 151; personality, 133
persuade, 38, 137
pessimism, 52, 77, 78, 79, 100, 101; pessimist, 52, 54, 73, 77, 78, 79, 84
philosopher, 3, 5, 6, 7, 8, 9, 15, 19, 23, 36, 37, 54, 66, 94, 97, 109, 153, 160; philosophical, 1, 3, 6, 7, 12, 14, 17, 18, 19, 20, 26, 36, 44, 49, 54, 62, 65, 92, 93, 154, 161; philosophizing, 82
physical, 53, 63, 65, 87, 88, 89, 145
Platonic–Aristotelian, 72
plausible, 87, 88
pleasure, 72, 88, 99
plutocrat, 105, 114, 117, 123, 124, 138
poetic, 44, 159
policy, 69, 71
political, 49, 69, 111, 112, 113, 115, 119, 123, 125, 137, 138, 144, 154
poor, 80, 117, 118, 119, 120, 121, 122, 128, 130, 132, 134, 138, 153, 154
position, 10, 22, 41, 42, 56, 157, 164
potentialities, 150, 153
poverty, 71, 117, 118, 120, 121, 131
power, 6, 22, 33, 42, 49, 54, 112, 118, 124, 129, 132, 135, 136, 138, 143
practice, 15, 49; practical, 15, 53, 57, 70, 71, 74, 77, 132, 138
predestinationism, 102
predict, 2, 74, 88, 90; prediction, 90

prehistoric, 88, 96
prejudice, 4, 24, 107, 122
prescriptive, 35, 36, 87
primacy, 11, 36, 47, 76
primitive, 87, 95, 96
principle, 29, 68, 104, 105, 108; principles, 6, 7, 21, 35, 41, 71, 119, 139
probable, 11, 13
problem, 8, 12, 15, 42, 59, 70, 71, 78, 89, 90, 118, 127, 130, 132, 136, 150
process, 9, 19, 20, 21, 46, 63, 75, 86, 87, 90, 108, 122, 139
produce, 47, 53, 79, 86, 119, 123, 132, 152; production, 47, 53, 61, 86, 129, 131, 132, 133, 134, 136, 152
professional, 9, 19, 23, 54
profound, 4, 12, 13, 15, 42, 47, 71, 74, 82, 95, 111, 116, 148, 155, 159; profundity, 1, 3, 12, 14, 37
progress, 71, 73, 74, 75, 78, 84, 101, 144
proof, 10, 22, 33, 47, 68, 99
propaganda, 11, 12; propagandist, 11, 23
prophet, 42, 90; prophetic, 38, 91, 109, 119
prove, 4, 10, 21, 34, 35, 41, 43, 48, 72, 73, 79, 81, 106, 159
psychological, 16, 18, 42
purpose, 12, 32, 65, 70, 74, 122

question, 5, 6, 10, 11, 12, 22, 23, 26, 28, 29, 34, 37, 39, 42, 44, 46, 53, 54, 56, 57, 58, 59, 61, 64, 66, 67, 71, 74, 75, 79, 80, 81, 84, 85, 115, 121, 123, 126, 128, 144, 156

rational, 10, 11, 14, 17, 19, 20, 21, 27, 28, 29, 30, 31, 34, 35, 39, 40, 41, 43, 44, 45, 46, 47, 48, 49, 60, 66, 68, 78, 82, 94, 109, 113, 145, 149, 161; rationally, 11, 44, 52, 113, 161; rationalism, 11, 21, 27, 28, 35, 38, 82, 85, 106, 147; rationality, 19, 26, 28, 29, 30, 39, 41, 42, 45, 46, 47, 82, 97, 109; rationalizing, 46
ratiocination, 19
real, 5, 6, 7, 18, 36, 37, 43, 48, 51, 58, 61, 68, 100, 101, 105, 151, 154, 157, 161; realist, 36, 58, 76, 78, 123; reality, 16, 18, 19, 21, 22, 26, 34, 36, 37, 41, 44, 47, 48, 55, 56, 58, 60, 75, 76, 89, 91, 93, 94, 99, 101, 106, 114, 117, 124, 133, 137, 147; reali-

zation, 20, 21, 52, 75, 76, 77, 78, 102, 150, 152, 157, 160, 165
reason, 1, 4, 9, 10, 13, 19, 25, 26, 27, 28, 29, 30, 33, 38, 39, 40, 41, 43, 45, 46, 55, 56, 60, 67, 68, 69, 70, 73, 76, 78, 80, 83, 94, 95, 97, 98, 102, 104, 107, 108, 113, 115, 117, 119, 133, 139, 141, 142, 144, 154, 157, 160, 163, 164, 166; reasonable, 29, 34, 41, 46, 49, 57, 58, 84, 97, 104, 105; reasoning, 6, 10, 19, 22, 29
reasons, 6, 7, 22, 27, 29, 40, 41, 46, 56, 65, 70, 92, 111, 120, 127
recognition, 28, 38, 53, 78, 142
reflect, 110; reflection, 7, 18, 19, 26, 116
reform, 77, 138; reformer, 78, 79, 84, 124
relation, 18, 30, 34, 37, 66, 75, 76, 120, 159; relationship, 38, 55, 75, 115, 125, 148, 151
religion, 18, 48, 61, 62, 66, 82, 91, 94, 95, 105, 108, 113, 153, 158, 159, 160, 161, 162, 163, 164, 165; religious, 18, 19, 20, 21, 26, 29, 33, 43, 44, 46, 48, 49, 66, 68, 82, 95, 105, 111, 112, 113, 114, 125, 129, 130, 148, 158, 159, 161
Renaissance, 145, 147
responsible, 39, 90, 95, 120, 138, 159; responsibility, 49, 51, 69, 82, 111, 148, 151, 154, 155, 162, 166
result, 2, 18, 46, 53, 67, 76, 158
revelation, 153, 154, 155
reverence, 114
revolution, 85, 131, 133, 138, 140, 141, 153
rhetoric, 82, 137; rhetorical, 31, 32, 38, 82
rich, 80, 117, 118, 123, 129, 130, 138, 142, 154
right, 15, 29, 34, 35, 38, 44, 56, 57, 58, 64, 71, 72, 74, 76, 79, 91, 112, 113, 115, 117, 118, 123, 131
romantic, 14, 76, 133, 139

sacrament, 127, 155
sacredness, 32, 111, 127
sacrifice, 38, 64, 155, 161
saint, 18, 114, 116, 140
sane, 11, 27, 48, 67, 137, 145; sanity, 11, 27, 35, 134, 137, 146, 166
satire, 86, 87
scepticism, 27, 55, 67, 78, 95, 100

scholars, 4, 7
Scholastic, 9, 53
science, 34, 35, 39, 67, 70, 83, 84, 85,
    88, 91, 95, 99, 109, 121, 135, 142,
    152; scientific, 35, 36, 64, 73, 85, 86,
    88, 89, 93, 99, 100, 106, 109, 110,
    115, 123, 162; scientist, 34, 87, 95,
    109, 110, 122
secular, 26, 90, 149, 157
see, 2, 7, 9, 10, 12, 18, 22, 39, 41, 44,
    45, 52, 54, 60, 69, 72, 73, 74, 76, 78,
    81, 82, 89, 90, 91, 100, 102, 114, 117,
    122, 123, 134, 135, 136, 138, 147,
    149, 159, 160, 166; seeing, 7, 9, 10,
    11, 18, 22, 41, 68, 72, 73, 90, 92, 99,
    152, 159
self, 17, 47, 48, 63, 70, 72, 113, 120,
    121, 124, 128, 148, 150, 152, 154
self-evident, 41
sensitivity, 17, 32
significant, 23, 37, 38, 55, 63, 70, 108,
    117
sin, 60, 101, 116, 154; sinner, 60, 116
social, 20, 49, 61, 64, 68, 69, 73, 76,
    85, 88, 109, 111, 119, 123, 125, 126,
    128, 130, 131, 137, 138, 140; so-
    cialism, 114, 117, 128, 129, 130, 131
society, 62, 64, 65, 69, 75, 76, 82, 91,
    111, 118, 120, 121, 123, 125, 126,
    127, 128, 133, 134, 137, 141, 148
solid, 21, 22, 30, 40, 56, 66, 163
solution, 32, 71, 137
sorrow, 78, 79
soul, 17, 80, 92, 155, 165
sound, 11, 29, 41, 66, 106, 154
source, 37, 47, 48, 50, 78, 86, 108, 113,
    158, 161
specifically, 6, 151
spirit, 19, 43, 45, 46, 47, 59, 76, 81,
    84, 88, 89, 91, 92, 93, 94, 95, 96,
    98, 103, 104, 106, 107, 108, 114, 134,
    140, 152, 155, 159; spiritual, 20, 47,
    52, 53, 54, 63, 66, 82, 83, 89, 92, 93,
    94, 95, 102, 103, 107, 124, 125, 133,
    134, 135, 140, 145, 155, 159; spiritu-
    alists, 93
stability, 62, 75
standard, 35, 68, 75, 76, 124
state, 90, 105, 118, 126, 127, 129, 132,
    133, 153
statement, 15, 31, 32, 40, 42, 43, 88
structure, 124, 128
student, 1, 2, 4, 5, 9
style, 1, 8, 9, 33, 38, 50

subject, 66, 99; subjective, 19, 66, 67,
    68, 69, 76, 82, 162
success, 72, 132
suffering, 54, 79, 160
superficial, 37, 76, 80
supernatural, 20, 40, 47, 84, 106, 108,
    114, 161, 165
superstition, 83, 84, 85, 94, 107, 108,
    158; superstitious, 2
suspicion, 14, 29, 86
synonymous, 10, 27, 49, 73, 87, 106,
    161, 165
system, 81, 87, 118, 119, 130, 132, 137;
    systematic, 7, 10, 11, 91, 129, 132;
    systematizing, 6

task, 8, 148, 150, 152, 166
teaching, 66, 102, 103, 104, 156, 160,
    163, 164
technology, 71, 85, 90
thankful, 17, 18, 80, 97, 98, 108
theology, 2, 18, 30, 81, 82, 95, 97, 151,
    164; theological, 19, 66, 153, 161,
    166
theory, 15, 64, 76, 86, 87, 88, 91, 93,
    122, 123, 124, 131, 132, 142, 149,
    158; theoretical, 70, 71, 132
think, 1, 4, 12, 20, 21, 27, 32, 44, 49,
    67, 68, 70, 74, 76, 79, 92, 133, 135,
    156, 161; thinker, 4, 13, 15, 23, 36,
    148
thought, 1, 3, 4, 5, 6, 8, 9, 11, 12, 14,
    15, 19, 20, 21, 26, 31, 37, 38, 40, 42,
    44, 46, 50, 53, 56, 58, 60, 62, 64,
    66, 71, 86, 91, 92, 94, 97, 102, 103,
    107, 108, 109, 111, 120, 123, 125,
    128, 132, 138, 139, 144, 149, 157,
    164
totalitarianism, 91, 126
totality, 18, 19, 37
tradition, 19, 43, 103, 113, 124, 152,
    157; traditional, 58
transcendence, 87
translation, 33, 56; translating, 33, 72
Trinity, 30, 153, 162
triplicity, 46
trivial, 3, 15, 55
true, 1, 4, 10, 13, 15, 26, 27, 29, 31,
    33, 35, 38, 39, 40, 41, 42, 44, 46,
    51, 55, 56, 58, 59, 65, 67, 89, 95,
    100, 103, 106, 108, 112, 115, 116,
    121, 125, 132, 143, 145, 152, 159,
    160, 162
trust, 151

truth, 11, 12, 18, 19, 22, 26, 29, 30, 31, 33, 34, 35, 38, 39, 41, 42, 43, 44, 45, 46, 49, 55, 60, 63, 65, 73, 78, 81, 86, 91, 93, 103, 113, 116, 117, 138, 145, 149, 154, 157, 158, 160, 161, 162, 163, 164
type, 71, 122, 123

understand, 8, 11, 25, 34, 56, 65, 70, 79, 89, 91, 93, 95, 102, 114, 115, 117, 121, 128, 145, 149, 152; understanding, 8, 19, 40, 47
universal, 15, 17, 35, 87, 113, 157
universe, 14, 26, 32, 34, 35, 36, 79, 133, 136
unreal, 51, 59, 157; unrealistic, 7, 60, 81, 134, 136
unscientific, 35, 85, 87
utilitarianism, 85

valid, 13, 76, 119, 150; validity, 29, 41, 65, 68, 88
value, 1, 44, 52, 54, 58, 66, 67, 69, 70, 75, 76, 78, 79, 111, 112, 116, 121, 124, 133, 143, 145, 148, 151, 157
Victorian, 61, 62, 82, 84, 144, 147

virtue, 17, 59, 61, 72, 81, 104, 121, 122, 139, 146; virtuous, 68, 69
vision, 8, 11, 48, 60, 154, 166
vocation, 33, 54

war, 12, 29, 60, 62, 91
wealth, 91, 117, 118, 121, 122, 128, 129, 131, 132, 138, 141, 142, 143
wholeness, 148, 150
will, 44, 53, 95, 98, 100, 101, 102, 140, 146, 154; willing, 1, 15, 44, 47, 139
wisdom, 8, 39, 41, 57, 85, 109, 124, 144, 150, 154, 166
woman, 115, 125
women, 29, 64, 144, 164
work, 128, 130, 135, 136; working, 53, 128
world, 12, 32, 36, 47, 48, 51, 52, 58, 59, 63, 77, 78, 79, 88, 101, 104, 108, 131, 144, 149, 153, 157, 161, 165
worthwhile, 3, 7, 15, 50, 52, 53, 54, 61, 78, 79, 101, 116, 137, 141
write, 1, 6, 8, 14, 37, 40, 128; writing, 2, 3, 9, 13, 20, 23, 25, 31, 40, 42, 45, 50, 65, 92, 111, 125
wrong, 48, 56, 57, 64, 72, 77, 79, 119, 130, 131, 165